MW01531812

The Writer's Path

Creative Exercises for Meaningful Essays

Charlotte Pence
Belmont University

KENDALL/HUNT PUBLISHING COMPANY
4050 Westmark Drive   Dubuque, Iowa 52002

Cover photos courtesy of Tia Goodman

Copyright © 2004 by Charlotte Pence

ISBN 0-7575-1086-8

Kendall/Hunt Publishing Company has the exclusive rights to reproduce this work,
to prepare derivative works from this work, or publicly distribute this work,
to publicly perform this work and to publicly display this work.

All rights reserved. No part of this publication may be reproduced,
stored in a retrieval system, or transmitted, in any form or by any
means, electronic, mechanical, photocopying, recording, or otherwise,
without the prior written permission of Kendall/Hunt Publishing Company.

Printed in the United States of America
10 9 8 7 6 5 4 3 2 1

This book is dedicated to my mother, Rita Blackwell Tate,
who will always be my first and best teacher.

About the Author
Charlotte Pence earned a B.A. from the University of Tennessee, Knoxville and a M.F.A. in Writing and Publishing from Emerson College, Boston. She has taught composition for seven years, the last six years at Belmont University in Nashville. In addition to teaching composition and poetry writing, her work has been published in a variety of journals such as *Southern Poetry Review*, *The Seattle Review*, and *Maryland Review*. In 2003, the Tennessee Arts Commission awarded her the Individual Artist Fellowship in Poetry.

Contents

Acknowledgments

No book is written by one person alone, and I want to express my gratitude to all of my colleagues who offered me support and wisdom: Bill Brown, Wyeth Burgess, Cynthia Cox, Sandra Hutchins, Alyson Muenzer, and Andrea Stover.

I would also like to thank my students who have taught me so much throughout the years. I especially want to thank those who allowed their work to be published in this book so that other young writers could benefit from their fine examples: Chris Beard, A.J. Bowley, Danielle Daunt, Lauren Hight, Brett Galli, Erica Grigsby, Janie Loventhal, Jennifer B. Moss, Samantha O'Keefe, Will Owen, Chris Rorie, Clayton Rothwell, Katherine Shelley, Alayna Sims, Kevin Smith, Shelby Thurman, Brianne Wells, and Clinton Wilson.

Despite my best efforts to thank my copy editor, Ginny Schutz, with chocolates and compliments, I will never be able to express the level of gratitude I feel for her professionalism and editorial insights. Without her, I would not have a book that I am as proud of as I am of *The Writer's Path*.

I would also like to thank the wonderfully supportive staff at Kendall Hunt particularly Emily Cabbage. I also feel a tremendous gratitude toward my associate editor, Stephen Perry, who has believed in this book from the beginning.

And finally, I would like to say thank you to all of my family and friends for supporting me and my choice to be a writer, wherever that path has lead. Of course, my husband deserves more than a thank you, and I try every day to show my appreciation for he has served as my muse and my allied critic for more than a decade.

With gratitude and respect, I am honored to have had such support from family, friends, and colleagues.

Introduction:
How to Use This Book

When I was six years old, I opened my brother's algebra book and started crying. I can still remember how my stomach tightened and my entire body stiffened. When Mother asked me what was wrong, I said, "X can't be a number! It can't!" Never, I thought, would I be able to understand my brother's text book. Yet five years later, I was captain of the math team. Yes, I had learned algebra, but, more importantly, I had come to understand that learning is a process.

Learning to write well is also a process. Although writing well may seem like a mysterious gift some people possess that others do not, writing can be learned, just like Algebra. On the first day of class, I tell my young writers that I expect drafts and many drafts. They groan, accustomed to writing an essay in one night and reading it over while munching on corn flakes the next morning. Revision? Drafts? Where is there time for this? In high school, I usually had three hours of homework a night, and the big projects and papers had to be done in addition to that. I never had time to do more than a draft or two, and consequently, I never felt like I improved my writing. It seemed like my essays always had the same comments and correction marks with only the color of the teacher's pen changing.

Writing is one of those skills where improvement only comes from correcting mistakes and problems. Simply writing and writing some more will do nothing but reinforce bad habits. For instance, when one learns piano, one does not improve by repeating the same mistakes but by forcing oneself to hit the right key.

Improving one's writing is done through reworking ideas and language draft after draft. This requires letting go of ideals and ego. For many students, being called "talented," "gifted," and "smart" has become more important than being called a "hard worker," when in fact being a hard worker gets better writing results than having innate ability.

Everyone can learn to write a great college essay. Everyone. My best writers are those who revise. My worst writers are those who believe they are already or innately good enough. Let me say this: you are never "good enough" at writing.

Writing is a process—and a long one at that. I've found that whenever I'm unhappy with my own writing, it is because I'm rushing to finish or to prove how good I can be. When I accept that every piece of writing can be better and that every piece of writing will have problems, I do not get tense about the work. I understand that through drafts, I'll work out any problems.

This book emphasizes the writing process, from the earliest stages of creation where one gets to feel as flighty as a dragonfly to the end stages of editing where a tight grip on the pen is demanded. I have divided the book into the four main stages of writing: prewriting, drafting, revising, and editing. Work through the book at your own pace. Do not feel obligated to do every exercise in the order listed. Skip around, work backward, work in circles, it doesn't matter—just work.

While you may skip around and do whatever exercise appeals to you within each section, adhere strictly to the book's section that reflects your essay's stage. For example, if you are just beginning to think about your essay, stay in the book's section on prewriting that addresses what to do at the beginning of an essay.

Below I have provided an overview of each section and its correlating phase. If you need to, refer to this section again as you begin writing your essay.

Section I: Developing the Writer's Mind

These exercises are designed to help you gain more confidence about your writing skills. You may use these strategies at any stage of the essay, beginning or end, or even when you aren't working on an essay at all. This section explains how to set up your work space and, most of all, perfect your writing process. This section also confronts writer's block, addresses potential critics, and explains how to build confidence in your writing.

Section II. Prewriting

As the name "prewriting" suggests, these are all exercises to do before you begin plunking away on your keyboard. This section focuses on finding a topic, exploring the general ideas that you want to discuss, and crafting a thesis statement. In this writing stage, the emphasis is on brainstorming, discovery, and creating.

Section III. Drafting

Use this section when you are writing your first or second draft of the essay. Exercises here will help you outline your points, find support for your position, and create the introduction and conclusion. Moreover, this section will help you deepen your argument and move your writing into more complex and unique areas.

Section IV. Revising

As the name suggests, this is the time for revising. Often students confuse revision and editing. The main difference between the two is that editing fixes little mistakes, mistakes that are more grammatical in nature or issues of word choice. Revising addresses the ideas and content of your paper. It means you are willing to take out large chunks of text or add more material. In the revising stage, you are still writing but have a solid draft that you want to sculpt into the final product.

Section V. Editing

The final stage! This is editing like you've never done before. Think of it as the finishing touches that an artist will do to a painting. In this section, you will learn how to make your writing more concise, more rhythmic, and more powerful.

Section VI. Appendix

This section provides a list of my favorite freewrites and some basic grammar rules. While the grammar rules explained in this section should not replace your grammar book, I have provided a chapter on the most frequently committed grammatical errors.

The exercises that follow in this book will be useful for writing the type of essays commonly required in first-year English courses: argument, research, and narrative type essays. Argument essays are those where you take a position and try to persuade the reader to your side of the debate. Research essays are quite similar to an argument essay with the addition of research. Narratives essays feature stories about your life, similar to autobiography. Most of these exercises will work for all three types of essays. When the exercise does not, I make a note of it.

With these exercises, I have two goals in mind: to improve your writing, of course, but more than that, I want you to enjoy the writing. I want what you write to affect you. In turn, I want your writing to affect others. For too long you have been writing essay after essay simply to complete an assignment. No more. This is your life. This is your writing. Do not waste this opportunity to use your creativity. Instead, use your college essays to reflect all of who you are. Your essays are another outlet for your creativity just like writing a song, decorating your dorm room, or dyeing your hair. College essay writing should not be void of your passions and creativity. Ultimately, the best essays are ones that combine what the professor wants with what the writer cares about. I have read research essays on drag racing, flip flops, and tattooing. While those topics may not seem "academic" enough, any topic which uses proper writing techniques that I explain in this book can work. It is time to make your writing, all of your writing, represent your uniqueness and creativity.

Section I

Developing the Writer's Mind

It's the Superbowl, and the score is tied with one minute left on the clock. Instead of being bored from watching a four-hour football game, you are riveted, watching as the quarterback has one last opportunity to make something happen. Every one knows what happens next will be as much about mental strength as physical capability. Will the quarterback get nervous and make a dumb mistake? Or will his determination to win gift him with the focus he needs to make the perfect play?

As with sports, writing requires a positive and healthy mentality. The exercises in the following section will help you get into the right mental space. Whether it involves finally resolving a criticism you received years ago concerning your writing or grappling with writer's block, the exercises here will give you the tools to write as well as you know you can, enabling you to throw right into the numbers on a windy day.

1
Bringing the Critic to Life

There will be time to murder and create,
And time for all the works and days of hands
That lift and drop a question on your plate:
Time for you and time for me,
And time yet for a hundred indecisions
And for a hundred visions and revisions,
Before the taking of a toast and tea.

—*From "The Love Song of J. Alfred Prufrock" by T.S. Eliot*

Today, I began the semester, and aside from the typical talk of future assignments and daily expectations, the conversation took a familiar turn. My students began to tell me how inadequate they felt concerning writing, how much they procrastinate, how they had never been taught how to write or had been taught by a red pen-wielding fiend. Essentially, they told me what their inner critic told them: they were no good. They could not write. Essay after essay in high school had only served as proof for this. On the first day of English class, I hear praise for subjects such as math which students claim has clear cut answers and rules ready for memorization—a subject free of the baggage that writing brings with it on any visit.

Why is it that writing can sometimes feel so discouraging? Most students believe if they cannot write well, they will never write well. Essentially, they feel they need to give it up and accept the "C" with a smile of gratitude. Yet, writing is not unlike other subjects where if the grades are poor, the solution is study more, party less. What is underneath all of this anxiety?

Part of the answer is that as writers, young and old, we listen too much to the inner critic. We block out the creator in our minds, that little voice that always raises its hand and asks for permission to speak, the one that loves to play and create. This is the voice that the first moment after a break-up looks for a pen to write a vicious poem. This is the voice that gets giddy at the idea of recording an album. This creative voice, however, often gets bullied out of existence by the critic. The critic will say, "What are you thinking doing an album of your own stuff? You can barely play the guitar." That critical voice can overpower and overrun the creative urge and basic desire to write. Some call this voice the inner critic. And that inner critic, while fabulous in certain moments such as wanting you to check for typos before turning in an essay, needs to be put in its cage until at least the second draft of your essay.

The problem is many of us don't even realize that we have both a creator and critic taking up dual residency in the mind. Sure, we talk of left-brained activities and right-brained activities, but we forget that perhaps we let one dominate more than it should, that perhaps it takes both sides in the proper balance to ever bring any project to fruition. Do the following exercise to help distinguish between the appropriate time for the critic's visit versus the inappropriate time for him to knock on your front door.

Exercise 1: Describing Your Critic

The first step in taming this critic gone mad is to admit that it exists. For this exercise, I want you to describe your critic in full detail. What does it say to you? When does it get loudest? Does it have a face? Is it just one person, perhaps Mrs. Burns from eleventh grade English class, or is it a composite of father, brother, friend, failed essay? Learn who it is, recognize how it speaks, and most of all, through this exercise, learn to imprison the critic in its imaginary home. I suggest that you name your critic so that you can talk directly to it. You need to silence your inner critic in the first draft of an essay when you need your thoughts to flow and your creative voice to speak.

Student Sample:
The critic inside of me says many different things at many times while I am writing. My critic probably gets most of its boundaries and judgmental attitudes from my own thoughts, but also from what I have heard from my mom and my high school English teacher. My critic gets way too loud when I try to begin or end an essay. It constantly will tell me that what I am doing will just not work. That is probably the reason I become very frustrated at the start and end of a paper. The critic in me is always checking up on me throughout the paper, but I think it is best that "Susan" remains quiet when I start writing.

—Lauren Hight

2
Mining the Past

We can travel a long way and do many different things, but our deepest happiness is not born from accumulating new experiences. It is born from letting go of what is unnecessary, and knowing ourselves to be always at home. —Sharon Salzberg

I'll break the stereotype of a poet and confess something to you: I love to watch sports. Notice, I used the word "watch" rather than participate. My reasons behind this pastime might differ slightly from my neighbor who has his beer club over every Saturday to watch the game and hit golf balls onto the roof of the chili factory down the street. The reason why I love to watch sports is because I like to witness someone pushing the body past what reason says it can do. I love to see that look of awe and disbelief and relief when a goal has been achieved. I can relate. When I finish a difficult poem or when one day I finish that novel I'm working on, I'll have that same look on my face. Always the athlete is smiling that smile of disbelief, wide and open, like that of a lottery winner. "I did it!" is what the thought must be.

Watching sports also reaffirms my belief that confidence is the key to success in writing. One of my favorite tennis players, Serena Williams, said in an interview in *Ebony* magazine that she doesn't believe that she dominates the sport because she is in great physical shape. She says that it's all confidence. When you think you can do something and everybody around you thinks you can, too, it's as good as done.

To write well, one must have confidence that one can write well. In order to have confidence, we need to address and fully recover from what has happened in the past that has made us doubt ourselves. What I'm talking about are experiences such as making straight "C"s throughout high school or getting a lower than expected score on the SAT, anything that made you doubt that you're a good writer or could be a good writer. Some writers call this overall negativity from past experiences regarding one's work creative scarring. Yet, creative scarring never needs to occur. For example, when you do accidentally cut yourself and properly take care of the wound, usually you do not have any scars unless it is a large wound. As writers, if we heal ourselves properly in the first place, which means fully acknowledging how we feel, then no scarring

5

occurs. Every now and then, I have to throw myself a pity party, and I put on pajamas in late afternoon, purchase Skittles and pizza rolls, watch TV and blab to whomever will listen how I'm an awful writer. Trust me. This gets old fast, and I'm over my problem after a good night's sleep.

Exercise 1: Back to the Future

Without regular pity parties, we could build up scar tissue. Four years of high school English always leaves some mark, I promise. For this exercise, I want you to list all of the negative experiences you've had with writing that have hurt your confidence. List all of them. Next, do something that will fully let them die. Burn the list, have a pity party, do a freewrite telling off those who wronged you, tell yourself how the past is the past. Whatever you do, address them and be done with them. Sometimes, you have to go back to the past and confront old enemies in order to move ahead with confidence.

Exercise 2: Successful Failures

Every writer, no matter how good he or she is, has a story to tell that could have ended the writing career. Here's mine:

that no one else could tell :

It was my junior year in high school and one of the first warm days of spring. In my hurry to get out of the building, I dropped my notebook and out spilled all my papers. I was in English class, and everyone bolted past me, leaving me alone with the teacher who simply leaned over her desk and watched me collect one shoe-marked paper after the other. Finally, I had placed everything back in the binder, and my eyes were on the door.

"Oh, Charlotte," she said. "I've been meaning to talk to you."

This teacher was one of those English teachers loved by many and disliked by few. I was part of this few. There she was, smiling down at me, but something made her tense, and so she kept fiddling with her necklace, sliding the charm on the thin gold chain side to side.

"I need to tell you a little something that I've noticed. You write for the newspaper. You're on the staff of the literary journal and wrote a lot of pieces for it, too. I'm not going to mention that other writing project you did, that little unapproved newspaper because I can't prove you were the one sneaking in the building at night, putting them in everyone's lockers. Anyway, the point is, you're involved in everything with writing at this school, and I just wanted to tell you—you're never going to be a writer. You're not that good."

I'm sure I mumbled something like, "Okay." I'm sure I moved out of there quickly as I could, and I'm sure I learned the exact temperature at which tears can feel like they are burning the eyes. But I have to tell you the truth. Soon as I stepped out of the building, I felt great. I felt a lightness enter a place inside me that I didn't even know had been weighing me down.

You see, I didn't like her. I felt like she couldn't teach writing better than a monkey at a zoo. So, I discounted her opinion which I must say you have to learn to do as a writer: quickly learn who to listen to and who not to. I was happy because I finally knew what I wanted to do with my life. I had no clue that I wanted to be a writer until she listed all the writing activities I was involved in. Once she did that, my anxiety over who I would be, what I would do, vanished. Writing was my life and would remain my life.

The other event that greatly affected my writing occurred my sophomore year in college. This English professor came to class early and put his bags down on the front table. Usually, he immediately unbuckled his bag and set out the class poetry book, but this time he looked straight at me. "Come with me to get a Coke," he said.

I felt my spine stiffen. "Here we go again," I thought. As we walked down the long hall toward the soda machine he said, "I don't know what you're planning on doing with your life, but it should involve writing. You are one of the most talented students I've had in years."

These two teachers taught me so many important lessons in writing. First, you won't have everyone's approval. Second, you will also be knocked down a couple of times—and hard—but what matters is how you respond to life's discouragements. With writing and with life, one has to see the positive in every negative situation such as when I listened to my high school teacher's list of how I involved myself in everything concerning writing rather than listening to her telling me to give it up. What gives me strength as a writer is knowing that I've overcome many negative situations in the past.

For this exercise, I want you to write about a negative experience you have had that you turned into something positive. If you'd like to just focus on writing experiences, that's fine. If you want to open this exercise up to your life, that's fine, too. Writing and life—they are interchangeable. These negative and painful experiences are often the inspiration for the most powerful and accessible writings. The intense emotion that results from these situations is a writer's reserve for authentic, original work.

Exercise 3: Positive Polly

For this exercise, list all of your positive past experiences with regard to your creative work. List any work that you were proud to have written or any work where others viewed it as successful. The goal here is to see what you have done well—and own it. For some reason, we love to diminish the positive experiences and focus on the negative ones. That habit can harm your creativity.

3
The Ultimate Writing Process

"Everyday's a brother to another," I once heard a coworker say. This was when I was sixteen and making cinnamon rolls at 5:00 a.m for extra spending money. Sometimes I'd be so sleepy, I'd forget the cinnamon. My coworkers tended to be older than I and accustomed to the hours, but still, they were tired from the monotony of working a minimum wage job fifty hours a week. They told it best: "Everyday's a brother to another."

Sometimes writers, young and old, approach writing the same way every day, essay after essay. I'm accustomed to getting up at seven and writing four hours. Then, I teach. I do this even if we have a freak snowstorm here in Tennessee, but to be honest, just because I'm used to writing in a certain way at a certain time doesn't mean that's always best. Every now and then, I need to break out from my daily routine and let myself dream.

Dreaming about what one wants out of life isn't exactly a well respected past time. As my uncle says, "Wish in one hand and spit in the other. See which one fills up first." Gross image aside, his "instructions" represent what many believe. Wishing for something doesn't make it so. Well, I disagree. Sometimes allowing our minds to expand and dream brings us to some conclusions we wouldn't be able to make in our day-to-day survival mentality. A lot of people think that college students are all about dreaming big, but most students whom I know are moving from class to class, stressed as can be, racing to finish assignments and then get on to their internships or part-time jobs. We all could use a little more dreaming about the ideal.

Exercise 1: Wish in One Hand, Act with the Other

For this exercise, I want you to dream about your ideal writing process. When I say process, I mean exactly that. How do you want to conceive an idea? Sitting in a coffee shop brainstorming or perhaps walking around, letting whatever inspires you, inspire you? How do you want to start writing the essay? Where would you like to write? Out in the woods with your lap top or in a dark room with the music blaring? How do you want to feel when you are writing? Excited, calm, confident, all three? How much time do you want to finish the essay before the deadline? How do you want to feel once you're finished?

Answer those questions and any others that you can think of.

Once you are finished writing about your dream process, prove my uncle wrong. Try to incorporate a few, if not all, of your ideas into your life the next time you write. For example, if you said you want to write every essay lying on a beach in Hawaii, try to make a portion of that come true. Lie outside in the sun when you write or buy a poster of Hawaii and place it over your desk. Try to make your dream writing process come true. I promise: If you enjoy the writing process, you will produce good work. So, dream big—and then act!

4
The Writer's Workplace

Long before I was a writer, I fantasized about the type of room where a writer would pen his novels. My dream was a round room, perhaps a tower within a castle filled with plants and books. Multiple windows looked out upon a forest that was alive with deer and rare hummingbirds that would hover at the window, looking in at me looking out. I suppose there was a notebook to write in. Obviously, the work wasn't the focus of my daydream.

Once I became a writer, the image changed. It went from the fairytale castle image to what I thought was realistic—a spare bedroom in a New York apartment. What I focused my imagination on was the writer, hunched a full eight hours over his desk, the fingers typing nonstop unless he had to go and make a sandwich.

What I craved with the New York image was the idea of total concentration, something I felt that I lacked. Finally, what snapped me out of my "realistic image" was a passage that I read in Stephen King's book on writing. He said that even he, every day, would be interrupted. A dentist appointment, a knock on the door, a question from his wife, etc. A real writer learns and understands interruptions, (a.k.a. life), happen.

It was then that I realized I had a writer's life and a writing room and never even knew it. My writing space is simply a desk that takes up one wall alongside the living room. I have a picture of my favorite tennis star taped to the computer. Next to the computer are files and files of what I need to write. When I write, all I can see is what I have planned on seeing. The writing that needs to be done, a picture of Venus, and a flower. I purposely have no windows. This is my space to work, filled with the practical, the inspirational, and the beautiful. It is nothing fancy, nothing that Hollywood would want to film. It is, however, real. Too often, I've known beginning writers who actually didn't write because they didn't think they had a room for it. A writing space is only to help you work, never to prevent your work. Try the following exercises to establish your writing space.

Exercise 1: Something Old, Something New

For this exercise, I want you to create a working space. Of course, I'm thinking a writing space, but I want this to be cozy and appropriate for all of the homework that you'll be doing. Reading and writing will be the bulk of the work, so set up something practical. What you don't have that you need, go buy. This is a nonnegotiable, as important as the sheets on your bed. Once you finish with the practical elements of your work space such as where it will be, I have some suggestions.

1. Make sure you have a cozy reading area. I would include a lamp that you like, some comfortable place to sit, and a table or hard surface for a notebook and coffee.
2. Place something in your work area that inspires you.
3. Place something in your work area that you find beautiful or interesting to look at.
4. Place something in your work area that you can fiddle with when you're stuck on a passage, like a smooth stone from a camping trip or silly putty.
5. Create a trigger that means now is time to work. For example, I always have a hot cup of tea which serves as my trigger on my desk warmed by a candle. After my one caffeinated cup, I switch to chamomile. The idea here is for you to instantly associate concentrating with your trigger object. (Refrain from anything fatty, sugary, or alcoholic. This can create problems later.)
6. Remove any object that may actually distract you from working like a telephone.
7. In the end, the workspace should make work easier for you. If this is not happening, change what you need to change.

Exercise 2: Writing Refuge

The roommate won't stop kissing her new boyfriend, the gal learning drums two floors up can't keep a beat, and the phone refuses to ring although you should have received a call yesterday to tell you if you got the job that you want. Face it. No writing will be written, or written well, in your dorm room on this day.

For days like the one I just described, writers need a second writing spot, one that will serve as a refuge. Also, many writers find it beneficial to go to this second place simply when they get stuck with their writing. For this exercise, find a back-up writing spot. Take whatever assignment you need to work on and venture out into the world searching for that ideal writing refuge. You may not need the writing refuge today, but on the day that you will need it, you won't feel like searching for it; so, take the time now and find your writing refuge.

5
Writer's Block

Not Writing

A wasp rises to its papery
nest under the eaves
where it daubs

at the gray shape,
but seems unable
to enter its own house.

—*Jane Kenyon*

I don't believe writer's block exists. Now that doesn't mean that I haven't had times when I didn't know how to proceed, times when I had absolutely no ideas, times when I didn't like anything I wrote and hated every tip of every finger that touched the keyboard. You might be saying, "But that's writer's block!" Here's the difference between my writer's block and everyone else's: I keep on writing.

Writer's block is actually the fear of writing badly. There is not an actual block like some people have in their arteries. With writer's block, you can still sit down and write. You learned to hold that fat red pencil when you were six-years-old, and you know how to make letters into words. Of course you can come up with something to say. It may sound as if you are actually six-years-old, but that's fine. You are overcoming writer's block with every bad word you write.

Everybody gets stuck. Do not give it a name and accept your diagnosis as if it is your doomed fate. Do, however, try to figure out what is wrong and take the necessary steps to move out of this normal, albeit uncomfortable stage as soon as possible.

Did I just say writer's block is normal? Yes. Any writing you do will have problems and moments where nothing is progressing. Just remember that for

"Not Writing," copyright 1996 by the Estate of Jane Kenyon. Reprinted from *Otherwise: New & Selected Poems* with the permission of Graywolf Press, Saint Paul, Minnesota

every essay problem, a writing technique can solve it. Writer Patricia O'Connor, author of *Words Fail Me*, offers this great analogy about writer's block. She says to imagine yourself on a drive through the country. You come to a washed out bridge and what do you do? Pull over and wait until the state highway department brings out the construction crew and rebuilds the bridge? No. You go around it. You move on, in a different direction than what was expected, but you move on.

Writers must overcome writer's block the same way a driver overcomes a washed out bridge. You find a way around the problem and never simply sit and wait for the problem to disappear.

Exercise 1: What's the Problem?

There are so many different types of writer's block and so many different causes for it, I cannot offer one solution as if it were a panacea. What I have done in this chapter is "diagnosed" a few of the reasons why writers get stuck and prescribed my version of aspirin. Next time you are having trouble with your writing, read all of the entries and see which category fits you. Then, do one of the suggestions to fix the problem and move around that washed out bridge.

THE PROBLEM: YOU'RE JUST STARING AT THE COMPUTER
The Solutions:
- Take a break. Ten to fifteen minutes of rest is what you need to keep you going.
- Go for a walk.
- Go do something inspiring like listen to a favorite song.
- Change your clothes.
- Shower.
- Clean something.
- Leave the house, maybe run an errand, but come back in fifteen minutes.
- Eat some fruit.
- Tell yourself to write non-stop for fifteen minutes and not to worry about the quality of your writing.

THE PROBLEM: YOU BELIEVE YOUR PROFESSOR WILL HATE EVERYTHING
The Solutions:
- Schedule a meeting and talk it over with your professor.
- List what you've been told is good about your writing.
- List what you like about writing.
- Make sure your topic is one that you care about. Write this essay with two goals in mind: pleasing yourself and following the requirements on the assignment sheet.

- List everything you think your professor might say. Then, logically talk it out with yourself. What is true? What isn't? What might you need to change with your writing to improve it?

THE PROBLEM: YOU'VE HIT A DIFFICULT PASSAGE IN YOUR WRITING
The Solutions:
- Move on to another page.
- Discuss it with someone.
- Write down the problem with plans to work on it the next day. The solution may be clear if you give yourself time away from the issue.
- Maybe you are moving in the wrong direction or are simply wrong. Wait a day and see if the section should be cut or taken into another direction.

THE PROBLEM: EVERYTHING BORES YOU
The Solutions:
Ask yourself if you've been doing a lot of creating or working lately? If so, you may have run out of inspiration and dried up your artistic well. Do something to get you inspired again and feel free to take from the following list.

- Read other people's work. This can be fiction, poetry, or student essays.
- Make a list of 10 things that make you happy. Do at least one of them.
- Go on a walk.
- Do something with a friend.
- Write a freewrite from a topic in chapter thirty-three of this book.

THE PROBLEM: YOU'RE BEING A WEANY AND DON'T WANT TO DO THE WORK
The Solution:
Sometimes writing is just not fun. Writing is work. Think of all those people who return to their jobs after their lunch break. Do you think the construction crew really wanted to go back to digging post holes? Was the secretary just dying to answer the phone and answer everyone's questions? Of course not, but they do it anyway. The difficult aspect to school work is that you have a lot of unscheduled time to do it. And you are the only disciplining force. Nobody will dock your pay if you don't write one more paragraph. In the long run, however, your grades will suffer if you do not discipline yourself. I suggest you set a time and make yourself write, no exceptions. (P.S. Bribe yourself if you need to. One hour of work equals one hour of ping pong or whatever it is that will make you do your job.)

THE PROBLEM: FEAR
The Solutions:
Maybe you're having problems because you are afraid that the piece might not be good or that you cannot write it. I have a few comments about that.

- One, understand that all work needs to be revised. Tell yourself that this is a draft and all drafts have some good elements and some bad ones.
- Two, you need to build your confidence. Do chapters one and two of this book.
- Confront the audience. Maybe you're scared of who is going to read this essay. Think of some way to make them less of a threat. Make friends with a couple of people in class, ask the professor or a friend to read a draft, etc.
- Ask your professor for samples of successful essays to see exactly what is expected.

THE PROBLEM: YOU'RE NOT MAKING PROGRESS
The Solutions:

I've seen too many friends stuck on their dissertations for years, never making any progress yet working constantly. Sometimes this happens to the best of us. Here are a few ideas to help you move on.

- Limit your research time.
- Ask, why you are still working on the same problem? What's the fear?
- Get a valued second opinion on what to do, and then do it.

THE PROBLEM: NOTHING SEEMS RIGHT
The Solutions:

- Ask yourself if this is the right topic for you. Do you need one that you care more about?
- Ask yourself if you are mixing the critic and the creator. Remember, if you bring in the critic too soon, you will indeed feel as if nothing is right and won't even get a draft written.

ONE FINAL WORD ABOUT WRITER'S BLOCK

All writers go through some form of writer's block. The key to quickly overcoming writer's block is to act despite the lethargy that you feel. Talk to other writers, write boring essays, or try every single one of the exercises in this chapter. The point is not to turn off your computer and walk away until you have a moment of inspiration. If you do that, writer's block wins.

6
The Reward System

In Judaism there is an old tradition that when a young boy first begins to study, the very first time, after he reads his first word in the Torah, he is given a taste of honey or a sweet. This is so he will always associate learning with sweetness. It should be the same with writing. Right from the beginning, know it is good and pleasant.
—Natalie Goldberg from Writing Down the Bones

My husband and I are training our puppy to act like she's not a puppy. We're teaching her how to stay seated on the floor throughout dinner, how to come when called no matter what her nose is sniffing, and how to keep all four fat muddy paws on the ground rather than on my silk skirts. My husband believes all of this training should be done with positive praise rather than food treats. We tried his way. Now, our cabinets are stocked with every funky-shaped, foul-smelling dog treat you can imagine. What's more, what was taking the pup a week to learn, and a long week at that, can now be taught in five minutes with a food treat.

When I think of what gets me through the tough work that I have to do, I always do better if there is some form of a reward at the end. How many times have I stayed awake the night before a beach vacation to get more work done? While we believe that doing the right thing should be reward enough, sometimes it is not. Let's face it. We're still puppies at heart.

Exercise 1: An Old-Fashioned Treat

I suggest that we use rewards more to get us to write what we need to write. For this exercise, think of a writing assignment that you've been procrastinating. Set up a specific time to write and a goal of what you want to accomplish during that time. Once you are finished, give yourself a treat.

Exercise 2: Trick and Treat

One of my colleagues read an article about exercising that explained if you could talk yourself into only exercising for ten minutes, and an easy ten minutes, then you would likely continue your workout because you would become engaged. Writing can work that way, too. On mornings I don't want to write, if I tell myself to start off with something easy for only fifteen minutes, I will usually get so involved, I don't notice the time until three hours later when that puppy of mine whines at the door for me to take her out. For this exercise, "trick" yourself into writing by agreeing to start off with something easy for fifteen minutes. If you end up writing longer, "treat" yourself with a little reward.

Section II

Prewriting

Have you ever planned to paint a room and were so excited to see the new color resuscitate drab white walls that you didn't prep for the job? I have. Once I bought two gallons of Sedona Sunset and First Day of Spring Green, and I wanted to paint immediately—and so I did. But the next day I realized I had splattered my bedroom suite (the one inherited from my grandfather) because I didn't cover the furniture, and I had streaked Sedona Sunset over the white windowsills because I didn't tape. Of course, I had to fix both of my mistakes which required razor blades and a new paint job to the windowsills. If I had only taken the proper time to set up, which I was too impatient to do, I would have saved myself hours of tedious corrections.

Sometimes we approach prewriting with the same, "Aww shucks, do I have to?" dread that we had as five-year-olds before bath time or twenty-five-year-olds before paint jobs. We know we should prewrite, but sometimes we don't want to do it or feel like we don't have time to do it; therefore, we dismiss it.

The truth is prewriting is far more than a "recommended" practice like letting a pan soak before you wash it. Prewriting, while it can sometimes feel like a waste of time in the beginning, will actually save you time in the end. But more than that, prewriting allows you to relax as you write. You should not feel any anxiety when you prewrite because you are only drafting, and drafting allows for mistakes, bad ideas, and out right goofy epiphanies. That's the point of it. As you read through the following chapter on prewriting, remember the point. All good writers prewrite. This is the time when your thoughts can flow and when your creativity can run unleashed. So, enjoy the prewriting and know that for every minute you prewrite, you have a minute less of agonizing edits.

7
The Best Form of Prewriting

Almost every writer I know leaves the house armed. We carry pen and paper with us no matter where we go. Here's an excerpt from a page of my notebook that is carried with me at all times:

—The old man's pendulous lips did not contain all of his saliva when he talked.
—For my advanced class, spend thirty minutes practicing sentence structure variety.
—Do I have a place for sacred things?
—Read: Letters to a Young Poet
—Grass weeds on the side of the road fall in an arc under the weight of their seeds, the possibilities just beginning.

Obviously, I do not have any works of art here. The line about the pendulous lips occurred because I was glancing at a bookstore calender that used that term, pendulous, to describe a dog's jowls. Maybe, I thought, I would need that description for a poem later. The same idea made me write down the image of the fallen grass. And the other notes are instructions to myself.

Whether or not I ever read or use what I write is not as important as the fact that I'm training my mind to look for inspiration and interesting details. I tried telling myself to simply remember that cool word, that snippet of funny overheard conversation, that poem idea, but invariably I would forget. Life moves by too quickly. Thoughts get hit out of the way by the next thought. Yet, carrying a notebook gives my creative side some space to record what I find interesting in the world.

If I confined my creativity to a couple of hours every few weeks when I need to write an essay, I can guarantee my creativity wouldn't be as strong as it is now because of my continual practice. Like anything else with our minds and bodies, one needs to practice to improve skills, and that works for creativity too. I know that many of the essays you write will not be full of lines about pendulous lips. No matter. What is important is that you're honing your skills as a writer by paying attention to detail and by being creative daily—both skills which are necessary to good essay writing.

Exercise 1: Carrying a Notebook

For this exercise, I invite you to carry a little notebook with you for one day to help you look for inspiration. Be open and aware to what is around you, what you're thinking about, and what you see. Write down anything that might be of use one day.

I also know some writers who don't carry around a notebook but who keep one religiously by their beds. They say that right when they wake up in the morning or right before they fall asleep, they have great ideas. Keeping a notebook on your night stand would also work well for your creativity.

Of course, the ideal goal is that you start carrying the notebook with you at all times, but begin by trying it for one day.

8
Generating Topic Ideas

Part of our duty as writers is to do the work of honestly determining what matters to us and to try to write about that. —Julia Cameron from The Right to Write

Finding a topic is either what students love the most about an essay assignment or what they hate the most. To the ones who love it, they see finding a topic as a time of great potential and possibility. But many students find that when a topic is demanded, the brain freezes as if another ice age has begun. Instead of killing dinosaurs, the freeze kills creativity.

I cause much panic in my class when I hand out assignments because I never provide the topic. My reason here is not to provide torture. Choosing a topic is an extremely important and critical choice in determining an essay's success. Most students know this—that's why the brain freezes on them.

So, why do I leave my students to fend for themselves? Choosing one's topic should be a personal decision. To write a good essay, the writer has to care deeply about the subject. If you don't care about the subject, there will remain a deadness to the essay, no matter how many somersaults your writing pulls off. This is one of the secrets to good writing: If you don't care about your topic, and care passionately, nobody else will either. As poet Robert Frost said, if there are no tears for the writer, there are no tears for the reader.

Seeing as how topic choice is so important, how does one get to the creative place where topics begin to flow? The trick to letting ideas flow is to go against conventional wisdom and avoid trying to "think something up." What I mean is that you should go inward and see what is already there, what is already occupying your thoughts rather than reaching out into the air and hoping to grasp the golden idea. To choose a topic idea, one must ask oneself, what is going on with me? What do I care about? What is a problem in my life? What have I been thinking about lately? This is not the time to bring in the critic. Instead, let all of your ideas speak. The reason why the brain freezes is the writer is being too critical, demanding something good and immediate. Nothing will bring an end to creativity quicker than harsh demands such as, "Come up with something good. And now."

Remember as you do the following exercises not to try to think something up, but go inward and ask yourself what is already there.

Exercise 1: Freewrite

I have to put this exercise in early because freewrites are the foundation to your writing. Consider freewriting to be to writing what stretching is to sports —necessary to perform well and necessary to prevent future problems. A freewrite is simply a set period of time when you force yourself to keep the pen moving across the page. The reason behind writing fast and furious is that you want to jump start your creativity and prevent the critic from chiming in. If you are a beginning writer, start with five minutes. Everyday before I write, I begin with a freewrite where I just write down whatever is going through my mind. Other times when I do a freewrite, I give myself a topic to write about. Sometimes I give myself a line to begin with and return to if I get stuck.

For this freewrite, write for five minutes on what has been going through your mind. Is it news of a possible war? Are you wondering what to do with your life after college? If your mind begins to think about how these thoughts could be shaped into a possible essay topic, that's fine. If what you're saying feels far from any potential essay, don't worry about it at this time. The idea here is to get down on paper what you've been thinking about.

Experiment to see what works best for you, but follow the following rules.

Freewrite Rules

1. Don't stop moving your pen, no matter what. (Yes, you may use pencil although I find lead to drag across the grooves of paper. And, yes, you may also type these.) Even if you have to write, "I don't know what to say," write that.
2. Don't worry about grammar, spelling, or punctuation. (Finally!)
3. Go wherever your mind takes you, even if this means off the topic.
4. Don't be afraid of what you say, who you might offend, or who might read this. The freewrites are yours alone, and you never have to show them to anyone.
5. Write until the time ends or until you fill up the designated number of pages.
6. Write Fast! Part of the idea behind freewrites is to tap into the subconscious. Moving the hand quickly across the page forces the critic to let the creator work.

Exercise 2: List Leads

Brainstorming is one of the best ways to come up with topic ideas. For one, if you do it quickly, forcing yourself to come up with anything, good or bad, the critic has little room to instill doubts. Below you will find a list of questions organized by type of essay that you may be assigned (research/argument or narrative/personal). Find the type of essay you are doing and answer the questions quickly as you can, providing at least three answers for every question. Remember: put down all your thoughts, stupid or otherwise. Also, do not worry about whether your answers will make for a good essay topic. The focus now should simply be on generation. Once you are through with answering the questions, move on to the next exercise which will help you angle your answers to make them more appropriate for a college essay.

Questions for a Research and/or Argument Essay:

1. What have you been thinking about lately?

   _____

   _____

2. What is a problem in your life that research or writing would perhaps help resolve? For example, is a parent sick with a certain disease that you need to research in order to find the best type of care? Are you thinking about becoming a vegetarian? Do you need to buy a new car?

   _____

   _____

3. What is perhaps too personal to write about?

   _____

   _____

4. What do you have a lot of knowledge about? Put down whatever this may be from cooking to hunting to playing a particular sport. Often, there are topics within these answers.

   _____

   _____

5. What has been upsetting to you in the news? Perhaps you could research the reasons behind a particular current event or write an essay taking a side to a current debate.

   _____

   _____

6. What have you always wanted to learn more about? This can be something as silly as Jennifer Aniston to something as serious as genetics.

_____

_____

7. What questions do you have about your future?

_____

_____

8. What do you care about passionately?

_____

_____

9. What could you teach your professor?

_____

_____

10. What other thoughts do you have for a good essay topic?

_____

_____

Now, circle your favorite answers and do Exercise #3.

Questions for a Narrative Essay:

1. List the five major points in your life that shaped your personality. By this, I don't mean tragedies or celebrations. If that is the case, fine, but feel free to look at what others might have considered insignificant.

_____

_____

2. What are especially vivid memories?

_____

_____

3. What have you been the most ashamed about doing?

_____

_____

4. What are some activities that you have done for a while that help explain who you are? For example, are you a singer, a beauty contestant, a writer?

_____

_____

5. Name some points in American history that you witnessed or actively participated in. Keep in mind that your sense of history may be different from others'. For example, did Kurt Cobain's death greatly affect you?

_____

_____

6. What would be a good topic, but maybe too personal?

_____

_____

7. What have you been thinking a lot about lately?

_____

_____

8. What is a problem in your life?

_____

_____

9. Provide a time in your life that challenged or changed your beliefs?

_____

_____

10. What ideas do you have for a narrative essay?

_____

_____

Now, circle your favorite answers. To make your ideas appropriate for your essay assignment, review your assignment sheet and see which one would work with the least amount of editing. Exercise #3 is written for an argument/research essay, but the ideas still might help you if you are writing a narrative.

Exercise 3: What Qualifies as a Good Topic?

PART A: GETTING YOUR TOPIC MORE SPECIFIC

The following exercise is best used for an argument or research essay. Once you have brainstormed already in exercise two, then you may bring in the critic. Let's say you are doing an argument essay and wrote down "football" as something that you've been thinking a lot about. Obviously, that is a big topic and needs to become more manageable to use for an essay. How can you whittle it down? I suggest that you ask yourself what questions you have about that topic. For example, what team will win the Super Bowl? Or, how can I pass the football better? Your essay would then answer that question.

If you were doing a narrative essay, look at what you circled as your favorite topics. Ask yourself, what would be the message that this essay topic would try to get across to the reader?

For each of your favorite topics, come up with one or two questions that an essay could answer.

_____

_____

_____

_____

_____

_____

_____

_____

PART B: CRITERIA CHECK LIST

Take your favorite ideas and see which one meets all of the requirements from the following pages. Probably, no one topic idea will automatically fit, so be prepared to edit a little or a lot. It's also a great idea to tell your professor your essay topic to get his/her response.

What Qualifies as a Good Topic?

1. THE TOPIC IS NOT BASED ON TASTE

You want to avoid all topics that can boil down to personal taste such as whether something is ugly, pretty, good, or bad. Taste, I have learned by having a tacky grandmother who wears heels and sweat suits, cannot be debated.

Bad Example: Picasso is a wonderful artist, one of the great geniuses of painting.

(The problem here is the opposition will say he's not all that great; you will say he is, and then, the essay becomes a cat chasing its tail. In other words, if the reader didn't agree with you before you wrote the essay, then the reader won't agree with you at the end of the essay.)

Better Example: Picasso's use of abstract imagery and color helped him to become one of the best known painters of all times.

(By giving the audience something with which to judge, abstract images and color, the essay now can be debated in terms of technique rather than taste. Also, the word "wonderful" is deleted. Try to take out all of those "taste based" words such as good and bad. Instead, say why something is good or bad to help focus your writing.)

2. THE TOPIC IS ARGUMENTATIVE

Everything you write is argumentative, meaning there is something you are trying to persuade the reader to do or believe. A topic will not work if it is so timid that you are really saying nothing. So, make sure that there are some people out there, sane people, who would disagree with you.

Bad example: The American government has some strengths and some weaknesses.

(Who would disagree? No one, and that's the problem. The essay would end up having no focus and saying nothing.)

Better: The United States' drug problem is still rampant and getting worse despite the government's efforts which means a new course of action needs to be taken.

(This one is much better because there is a specific position taken—and therefore, it's more argumentative.)

Bad example: Movies today include racially diverse casts.

(The problem here is after one page, you will have nothing to write about because this is an observation. It is true.)

Better example: While movies include more of a racially diverse cast, the type of roles minorities play often reinforce negative stereotypes.

(See the difference? This one is an argument. Now, the essay has something to discuss.)

Another point I would like to make here is not to be too quick to discard a topic because it seems like there is no argument. Try to angle it so that you can make it argumentative. How you do this is by designing a question that your essay will try to answer.

Bad example: Tennis is a sport I love to do and is important to me.

(There's no argument here. Therefore, the essay will fall back to arguing about taste and only preach to the choir. For this example, ask yourself why do you love playing tennis?)

Better example: Tennis provides a cardio workout, strength training, and helps one to develop confidence which is why I love it and play daily.

3. THE TOPIC IS ONE YOU HAVE THE AUTHORITY
AND TIME TO ARGUE EFFECTIVELY

This rule requires that you look honestly at your schedule. I would not recommend topics that require your own science lab and decades of work such as what would cure AIDS. A topic, however, that researched the drugs already available to AIDS patients would work fine as long as you word the topic as a question to provide an argument. For example, discussing how close scientists are to curing AIDS would be a good topic.

4. DO NOT CHOOSE A TOPIC BASED ON CIRCULAR REASONING

What this rule means is do not require the readers to agree with a portion of your argument that you have no intention of arguing in order for them to agree with the entire essay. An example is best to explain this point. A poor topic would be one that wants to prove aliens have already landed on Earth. First of all, the writer is assuming everyone believes aliens exist, and one must believe that before one could entertain the idea of whether or not aliens are living in New York.

Issues of faith also fall into this category. Unless you are writing for an audience that is strictly adhering to one ideology, trying to convince someone that a certain God exists in a four page essay cannot be done. Could your faith be changed by reading a four page essay? Of course not. Also, do not choose a topic where your main argument is supported solely by the Bible or another religious text. If one doesn't already believe in a faith that finds guidance from the Bible, the support from the Bible won't be persuasive. Also, with so many different religious groups that study the Bible, one cannot assume one's interpretation will be another's interpretation.

5. THE TOPIC IS SPECIFIC

As soon as you can, narrow your topic so that you can cover all the necessary points. When an essay topic is too broad, you risk mentioning points that you cannot fully develop and prove. For an essay, trying to debate too broad of a topic will often hurt your grade far more than debating too narrow of a topic.

Bad example : I am against gun control.

(The problem is that gun control is a big issue with many components.)

Better: I do not support the addition of any new gun control laws such as the Brady Bill.

Overall, finding a topic should be a personal search with the goal being to find a topic that will improve your life after you write it. You may be skeptical that a college essay can do that, but as a professor, I have seen it happen more times than not. When my students decide to find a meaningful topic, they find it.

9
Topic Development

Now that you have a topic and can breathe a sigh of relief, allow your creative instincts to roam freely. I have a favorite Zen expression that relates here: "To tame a wild horse, give him an open field." Translation? To figure out what your essay will say, tell yourself that you can go anywhere you want with your topic. In the end, you'll find the right path for your essay faster than if you try to write an outline five minutes after conceiving the topic. The best essays are often those where the writer allowed himself some freedom instead of immediately trying to decide and limit what the essay could talk about. The following exercises are designed to help you explore your unique voice and to help you shape your essay into something a little different from what the professor has seen before.

Exercise 1: Looping

This exercise has a few different steps. Give yourself 20 minutes to do the entire exercise and follow along step by step.

Step One
Do a five minute freewrite on your essay topic. (For freewriting instructions, review chapter eight.) Write about what you want to say in your essay

Step Two
Read your freewrite and underline your favorite sentence or phrase from it.

Step Three
Beginning with your favorite sentence or phrase, do another five minute freewrite. The idea here is to focus on that favorite sentence or phrase and explore the idea more.

Step Four
Read your freewrite and underline your favorite sentence or phrase from it.

Step Five
Again, begin a new freewrite from your favorite sentence or phrase. Again, reflect on the meaning behind that good sentence or phrase.

Step Six

Take a look at everything you wrote and jot down some ideas of what you want to include in your essay. When you read the student sample below, notice how her argument deepens with each new freewrite.

Student Sample:

Freewrite #1: I believe that it is very important for everyone to learn a second language. It very much annoys me that English is sometimes viewed as the superior language. Other countries take the time to learn English, and I do not see why we should not slightly "inconvenience" ourselves and learn another language. I personally am drawn to Spanish. There are many Spanish speakers who continue to move into America. It is not only a thing of convenience, but also of courtesy to be able to communicate with these people effectively. Maybe if we were not so intent on the importance of our own language we would take the time to embrace another.

Freewrite #2: It is not only a thing of convenience, but also of courtesy to be able to communicate with these people effectively. Understanding a foreign language may also further the understanding of a culture. The French are often regarded as rude, but perhaps it is the attitude of those visiting France that needs a change. One must be willing to meet others where they are at. If this means both parties learning even just a small bit of another language, it can be a great benefit. We require most students to take a foreign language in high school or college, but it is most often done begrudgingly. One may learn just enough to get by, only because it is a requirement or one may take it upon himself to truly learn and begin instituting a change from within.

Freewrite #3: Understanding a foreign language may also further the understanding of a culture. The United States is an extremely diverse nation. It is inhabited by those from many countries and multiple backgrounds. In order to understand one another, one must be able to communicate. As a requirement for citizenship, the U.S. requires one to learn some English. I think one ought to be able to helpfully communicate with non-English speakers as they also learn. We often claim to be a tolerant nation, but there are many who still express an intolerance for non-English speakers and demand that the foreigners learn "our" language. If we are going to insist upon these standards then we also must live up to them.

-Erica Grigsby

Exercise 2: Dialoging

When my niece was three, her grandmother asked her what she wanted to be when she grew up. "I want to be a talker. I'm good at that," was her response. Everyone laughed, but I thought what she said was astute. She was an excellent talker—still is. And she should go into a career, perhaps broadcasting, that would benefit from her gift.

What my three-year-old niece realized was that being able to talk well is a talent. Maybe it is being shushed for the first eighteen years of our lives, but many people, for whatever reason, don't give talking the respect it deserves.

I consider talking about one's writing to be one of the best forms of writing. Yes, I realize there is a contradiction; if one is talking, one isn't writing. But to realize what we want to say, often times we have to fumble around, verbally, to get there. Many people will just fumble on the page. That's fine, but I find it is easier, and quicker, to simply talk about what I want to write about. What would take a few drafts of writing, I can solve in five minutes of talking.

For this exercise, find your roommate, call your mother, or bother your coworker and just talk for five minutes about your essay. Do this right now. (Your professor or a classmate are two of the best dialogue partners.) Begin by asking your partner if he would mind listening to you talk about your essay and invite him to interject his opinion. (You know people love to do that.) I also suggest you have pen and paper with you because at the end of your conversation, you'll want to record some thoughts.

Some possible questions you can ask your dialogue partner are: What is one point about my topic that I must address? From what I have discussed, what do you think is the main idea of my essay? What would you compare my topic to? What sounded like my strongest point as I talked? What is my weakest point?

Exercise 3: Moving Meditation

In the previous exercise, I mentioned the importance of talking about your essay. Here, I want to affirm the importance of simply thinking through your essay before you begin. This may sound like a no-brainer, but I can't tell you how many times students have moaned, "I haven't even started—and it's due tomorrow!" They say this as if their plane is going down in the Indian Ocean, and there is simply no salvation. I always calmly ask, "Have you thought about it?"

"Of course," they say.

"Well, then you've started."

That's the truth. Professors know that you learned the alphabet before you were five. We're not asking you to write an essay to see if you know English. We're asking you to write an essay to see if you know how to think.

For this exercise, whenever the topic comes to mind, allow yourself to think about it. Don't rush it away and stomp your foot as if you don't want to be bothered with that flea-ridden stray cat. Stray thoughts about the essay are actually gifts, little moments of inspiration. Write any thoughts down so that you can later incorporate them into your essay.

Perhaps you are the type who will never think about your essay until you make yourself. For you, I suggest a trigger which is an act that sends a signal to your mind that now is the time to think about your essay. For example, whenever you walk to the class where the essay is due, tell yourself to think about the essay during that walk. (Keep your head down so you don't get distracted.) I call this a moving meditation, and I must say, all writers do this. We often garden, walk, run, and knit because silent activities that require repetitive movements stimulate creativity. Scientists are now doing studies and discovering what writers have always known: Repetitive motions in silence trigger creative and complex thinking.

Exercise 4: Wash, Rinse, Repeat if Necessary

Another useful topic development exercise is to combine the three previous exercises. For example, write notes after your dialogue session, and then find one line to use for a freewrite. With that freewrite, begin looping. At the end of your looping exercise, take your favorite line and meditate on it as you do an activity like walking. Like the back of your shampoo bottle instructs, repeat if necessary.

10
Thesis Development

A thesis, a thesis, a thesis. This is what every college professor is going to say you have to have in your essay. So, what is a thesis? Some people describe it as an organizing idea, "The Big Idea," from which all your other ideas will stem. Some describe it as your main argument, your point. Simply put, the thesis is one sentence early in your essay, preferably the last sentence of your first paragraph, that says in a clear and concise manner what you will be trying to prove in your essay. Although the thesis ultimately helps you focus the essay, the thesis tells your reader early on what your essay is about and what your position is on the topic. And you must communicate this message in one sentence.

Another way to view the thesis statement is with the following idea. One of my colleagues has her class imagine that they have been selected to research on a specific crisis for the president. After hours of research and deliberating on the topic, she says to imagine being asked to speak to the president and tell him in thirty seconds or less what he should do. This reduction of ideas and opinions would be your thesis.

Below are some methods to help you create a thesis statement. Make sure you have decided on your topic idea before you try to formulate your thesis because you need to know your general topic before you can determine your stance concerning that topic. (If you need more work on topic selection and development, refer to chapters eight and nine.) Your initial thesis doesn't have to be perfect, but you need some sort of "working thesis" to provide direction as you construct your essay.

Exercise 1: What Qualifies as a Good Thesis?

What qualifies as a good thesis is quite similar to what qualifies as a good topic. Here are some guidelines that you should use to make sure your thesis statement is solid. If your thesis doesn't fit one or more of the following criteria, rewrite until it works.

A good thesis statement should be:

1. Argumentative. You want somebody in your class to be able to disagree with it.
2. Specific.
3. Not based on circular reasoning. In other words, do not require your reader to agree with an element of your essay that you will not be arguing. For example, do not say that divorce is wrong because the Catholic church disapproves of it. You are requiring your readers to be Catholic, and to agree with that particular viewpoint, to agree with you.
4. Clear and concise. Here is the one sentence of the entire essay that may be boring. What is crucial is that everyone knows what you're saying in your essay.
5. A statement, not a question. Often, students will phrase their thesis statements as questions. Don't do that. This is too important of a sentence to have your readers determine the answer.

Exercise 2: Practice Makes Perfect

For this exercise, practice writing thesis statements for the topics that I have provided. Remember to use all of the criteria from the previous exercise.

1. Gun control

_____

_____

2. College sports

_____

_____

3. Grade inflation

_____

_____

4. Abortion

_____

_____

5. Freedom of Speech

_____

_____

Exercise 3: Playing Professor

For this exercise, I want you to play professor. Below, I've provided some actual thesis statements from essays I've received. Rate them excellent, fair, or poor. Provide reasons for your mark and then check your answers with my answers at the end of this chapter. The goal here is to get your snout developed to sniff out weaknesses in other people's thesis statements so that you can detect flaws in yours.

Thesis Quiz
(**Note:** Any or all grammar mistakes have been left in these thesis statements.)

1. The conclusion that I have reached is that homosexuals' sexual preference is ethically wrong.

_____

_____

2. Hollywood is finally letting overweight women thrive in front of the camera as hosts, actors, and even models.

_____

_____

3. Although we do not want to impinge on the press's freedom, protected as it is by law, we don't want the press impinging on the rights of individuals, even public servants.

_____

_____

4. Sports figures are heavily imitated by children, and because of this, they should be accountable for them.

_____

_____

5. Although sharing this act of love with someone before marriage has become a popular habit, is it wrong and extremely consequential?

_____

_____

6. Because I myself was home schooled through the age of sixteen and attended public school to graduation, I can objectively state that home schooling is a very effective approach to education.

_____

_____

7. Although I would never burn our nation's flag, there should be no law that restricts this act protected as it is under our first amendment rights of freedom of speech.

_____

_____

8. Violence in our society can be directly linked through studies to violence in movies.

_____

_____

9. If society knew the pragmatic as well as moral facts of capital punishment, it would be viewed as unfair, inhumane and definitely discontinued —as it should be.

_____

_____

10. Although racism is a major issue in the United State that is often ignored, it is above and abundantly in our country today.

_____

_____

Answers to the Quiz

1. **Fair.** This thesis needs to be more specific. Instead of saying a word like wrong or bad or harmful, say instead how it is wrong or bad or harmful.
2. **Poor.** This thesis needs to be argumentative. As of now, it is an observation, and the essay will have nowhere to go.
3. **Excellent.** It follows all the criteria.

4. **Fair or Poor.** The problem with this one is that it is unclear. As it is worded, the author is arguing that Tiger Woods should be accountable for a kindergarten class going to the circus. Obviously, that's not what the student wants to say.

5. **Poor.** This needs to be more specific, clearer, and turned into a statement rather than a question. For one, we have the words "wrong" and "extremely consequential." Say how it is wrong and what would be the consequences. Also, to make it clearer, take out phrases such as "this act of love" and say premarital sex. Imagine that your thesis statement will be on a billboard to make sure it is 100% clear.

6. **Fair.** It is argumentative and clear, but could be more specific and concise. If the writer answered briefly why home schooling is better, it would serve to focus the essay.

7. **Excellent.** It follows all of the criteria.

8. **Excellent.** It follows all of the criteria.

9. **Fair.** The tone suggests that the world would agree with the writer if only the world were educated correctly. False assumption. Most people have good reasons for their beliefs. Also, because of overuse, I advise students to avoid using the word "society" to begin a thesis or essay.

10. **Poor.** The mistakes are making it unclear. Also, this thesis may not be argumentative enough. The following is a good example of a revision: Although many feel as if African Americans no longer face job discrimination, many studies show otherwise.

Exercise 4: Thesis as Question and Answer

For this exercise, I want you to ask yourself what is the main question your essay is trying to answer. For example, if your essay topic is about college athletics, what exactly is the question that you want to explore? Should college athletes receive lower admission standards? Should athletes receive money to play in college? Should there be an equal amount of scholarships for men's and women's teams?

In the space provided below, write down the question your essay is trying to answer. Once you have the question, answer it in a complete sentence providing a reason for your answer. This is a thesis statement, at least a working one, to get you started. Feel free to edit it later.

Sample:

1. What is your essay topic?

Gun control

2. What is the question your essay is trying to answer? Be specific.

Should there be stricter laws?

3. What is your answer to the question? Provide some sort of reason for your answer.

No. We need to enforce the laws we have and not add any new ones.

4. Write down your answer in a complete sentence. This is your working thesis.

For effective gun control, we need to enforce the established gun laws rather than create new ones.

Your Turn:

1. What is your essay topic?

_____

_____

2. What is the question your essay is trying to answer?

_____

_____

3. What is your answer to the question? Provide some sort of reason for your answer.

_____

_____

4. Write down your answer in a complete sentence. This is your working thesis.

_____

_____

Exercise 5: The Although Clause

This is a formula that usually produces some good results—and it's easy! Simply fill in the blanks: *Although (Put the opposition's viewpoint here.)*, *(Put your viewpoint here.)* .

Sample #1:
Although (many believe that separation of church and state diminishes religion's influence) , (the law actually protects religion from the government's influence).

Sample #2:
Although (many believe that violent movies create a violent society,) (no studies can conclusively prove that violence seen on the screen influences people's behavior).

Your Turn:
Although _____

_____

Exercise 6: X, Y, and Z

This type of thesis can help you organize your essay. State your position and then at the end of your thesis provide the reader with the three main reasons for your position. Your essay will then be structured according to those three reasons. The benefit with the X, Y, and Z thesis is that it provides you with a structure, yet this type of thesis statement can be overused.

Sample #1:
High school seniors should take a year off of scholastic study before college and travel so that they can mature, discover new interests, and learn in an environment outside of academics.

Sample #2:
Before I traveled to Haiti, I did not understand the reality of poverty, chaotic governments, or homelessness.

Your Turn:

_____

_____

11
Identifying Other Perspectives

We've all heard the expression that you are only as strong as your weakest teammate. In essay writing, the adage should be that you're only as strong as your opposition. What I mean by this is that every essay writer must understand completely and honestly what the opposition thinks. If the writer doesn't know the opposition, the writer essentially doesn't know what to write about. To avoid a one-sided and naive argument, writers must address the opposition. After all, persuasive essays are not written for those who agree with you, but for those who don't or who are undecided. Therefore, the opposition's views are as important for the writer to explore as his own.

Many young writers are hesitant to include the opposition because they fear that by stating someone else's thoughts in the essay, the reader will say, "Hey, that sounds like a good idea. I think I'm going to agree with that other opinion." Here's the deal: if the reader disagrees with you, he is already wondering about the point that you mentioned. You have to mention it so that you can refute it. By entering the opposition's arena and pointing out the holes in their argument, you thoroughly convince a skeptical reader.

Also, do not be afraid of a strong, legitimate opposition. In your essay, you want an intelligent opposing voice, one with credibility, facts, and clear opinions. The stronger the opposition sounds in your essay, the stronger you sound because a strong opposition helps you refine your argument and discover your illogical points. How does it work? Put in the opposition's very best points—and then refute them. If you put in exactly what the opposition would say if they were talking to you, exactly as the opposition wish they could say it, and then you effectively counter their points, your argument becomes strong and thorough. If you are writing a narrative essay, you still must address the opposition, although it will be different from how an argument essay addresses it. For example, if you are writing an essay about a car wreck that you say was not your fault, present how the other car's driver would view the situation. Even in a narrative, the opposition can help add depth, because you will address how your experience could be interpreted differently.

One of the more difficult tasks for students is exploring the opposition. This research, however, is one of the writer's more critical tasks. Knowing what the opposition will say is crucial to any good argument. Here are a few exercises to help get you there.

Exercise 1: Practicing with a Dummy

Imagine what the other side would say. To do this exercise, first decide where you stand on the issue. Then think of the two main reasons why someone would disagree with you. Remember, you want to record the opposition's best points and prepare to answer them. The last two topics in this exercise would be ones found in a narrative essay which still requires some type of opposition. Remember that in a narrative essay, the opposition provides a different perspective on your topic.

1. Premarital Sex

   _____

   _____

2. Term Limits

   _____

   _____

3. Prayer in School

   _____

   _____

4. Finding One's Religion

   _____

   _____

5. Falling in Love

   _____

   _____

Exercise 2: Targeted Freewrites

1. Do a ten-minute freewrite taking the opposite stance you are planning to take in your essay. For ten full minutes, try to persuade your own self. Once you are finished, underline the best points in the free write and incorporate them into your essay.
2. Do a ten-minute freewrite on the exceptions to your argument. In other words, under what conditions and scenarios are you incorrect? For exam-

ple, most abortion opponents concede the necessity of the procedure for rape, incest, and the mother's life. To not recognize and concede the reasonable exceptions will undermine your argument's impact. The reader will be distracted by thoughts like "But what about . . ." and will be less likely to consider your other points.

Student Sample:
(Notice how in this excerpt the writer's doubts serve as his opposition. In this essay, he is discussing his career choice.)
The problem lies in that the majority of actors are not making enough to live on. An aspiring actor could always join a union and be guaranteed a minimum of $125 per performance (Actor, SigiPlus 5). The downside to joining a union, however, is that there are many actors working for free to get their names recognized, and a studio or theater may be reluctant to hire an actor that must be paid.

—*Kevin Smith*

Exercise 3: Surf the Web

If you have no clue what the other side would say, search the Internet. If you know of groups that disagree with you—middle-of-the-road groups, not extremists—visit their sites on the Web. Avoid extremists because their opinions are too easy to discredit. For example, one student was writing on equality for men and women and used information from a site that promoted death to all men. His opinion, nevertheless, was more mainstream: Men and women are different, but deserve equal treatment. Having proponents of mass murder serve as your opposition will not help anyone. You won't address the thoughts your readers are thinking, and you are also wasting people's time arguing why we should not commit murder. Credible sites, though, can help you find some good opposition, so take a few minutes and explore the Internet.

If you don't know how to begin your search on the Internet, place "anti" in front of your topic and then search on Google.

Section III

Drafting

Now that you have your topic defined and developed, you are probably so excited to get your ideas down that you aren't even reading this paragraph; or you may be mildly dreading the task, feeling like an old car on a cold, winter day, hesitant to start. If you are the latter, you might be putting too much pressure on yourself. This stage of writing is called drafting. The word itself implies there are many drafts to come, so do not feel pressured to write something "good" the first time. This writing stage is about exploring and trying new ideas, so relax and try the following exercises.

12
Organizing Your Thoughts (a.k.a. Outlining)

Writer Carl Hiaasen swore that after college he never would outline again. I went through a similar period where I believed that my writing would have more energy if I allowed everything to flow organically rather than being forced and predetermined. After I wrote an entire novel "organically" and had to rewrite it with this little thing called an outline, I now disagree with my self.

But before we begin talking about organizing your thoughts, I want to do away with your old notion of outlining. You do not need to bring out your knowledge of Roman numerals if you don't want to do that. While not using an outline didn't work for me, neither did the Roman numeral outline with the "A must have a B" rule. What I have learned is that there are many different types of outlines that I can use, ones that still allow for creativity and flexibility, yet provide organization.

The type of outline I encourage is whatever works best for you. If it is scribbling some ideas of what to say on a post-it-note, wonderful. If it is doing a big, color-coded proposal suitable for a business meeting, fine. The point here is to save you time and agony later. That's all an outline should do: save you time and help organize your thoughts.

In this chapter, I have provided a few different ideas of how an essay can be organized. Do what seems to work the best for your topic. If you have some sort of organizing system that works well for you, do that. What is important here is that you organize in some way before you jump into the water, other than hold your breath and hope the water doesn't feel so cold.

For most of the assignments in college, you will need an outline, because let's face it, we don't always know what we are doing or where we are going with our writing. I know that two camps exist here, the outliners versus the non-outliners. Let me say this. If you are doing a short essay and if you have a clearly defined argument and if you know exactly what you want to say, an outline may not be necessary. Notice, however, there are a lot of "ifs" in that sentence. For the majority of your essays, try one of the outlines suggested in this chapter.

49

Exercise 1: A Basic Outline

Answer the following questions before you begin writing your essay. Then, organize your answers in a way that will help you write your essay. This exercise works best for an argument or research essay.

1. What is the main argument of the essay?
2. What are your five best points that would persuade someone?
3. What are the five strongest points against you?
4. Take out the weakest points in # 2 and #3.
5. Now, review what you have and see if any of your points should be linked together in the same paragraph or section.
6. Rewrite all of this information into a form that you can follow as you write. I recommend some type of outline that tells you the following:

   • The order of the paragraphs.
   • The focus of each paragraph.
   • An introduction paragraph with your thesis.
   • A conclusion paragraph.

Exercise 2: General Guidelines

Although essays are like snowflakes in that no two are alike, I can provide some general guidelines for an essay's structure. Review the list and write a rough outline according to the following general guidelines.

1. Provide an introduction first.
2. In your introduction, provide a thesis statement.
3. If you need to define your key terms or provide a "road map" for your essay, do so in the second paragraph.
4. The body of the essay begins with your strongest point.
5. As you finish the body of the essay, you end with another strong point.
6. Each paragraph features one main idea that is clearly stated in the paragraph's topic sentence.
7. You should have at least one paragraph that describes another person's perspective.
8. Provide a conclusion.

Exercise 3: Lead with the Opposition

*This exercise works best for an argument/research essay.

On Saturday when I write my errand list, I will force myself to complete the errands I don't like first and then do the fun ones last, like visiting the pet store. The reason, of course, is to ensure that I do what I'm supposed to do.

For this exercise, I suggest you address the opposition's issues first. Writing about the points you feel strongly about is the easy part. Answering the opposition is often the hardest part, so conquer it first. Not only will you take care of one crucial element, but you will also write an effective essay. For example, when people debate, both people care greatly about being understood; perhaps they care more about being understood than they do about learning the other person's point of view. This is understandable. We need to understand one another so that we can understand exactly the point of contention in order to reach any sort of resolution. So, structuring the essay with the opposition's views ensures that the opposition knows you understand them.

For this type of structure, come up with the opposition's main points against you. Beginning with the first paragraph of the body (which will usually be the second or third paragraph of the essay), have the topic sentence be the opposition's point. You will need to provide a few more sentences clearly explaining the opposition's position. Then, refute the opposition's argument by providing your facts. Once the opposition's point is fully explained away, which may take more than one paragraph, begin a new paragraph with another of the opposition's points. Continue writing the essay leading with the opposition's views and then refuting them.

Student Sample:
  (The following sample features only three topic sentences, but notice how she leads with the opposition's views. After the topic sentence, she then explores the opposition's view with facts and then refutes their idea with facts to support her position that the death penalty is unconstitutional.)
  Topic Sentence #1: It is often argued that death is what murderers deserve, and that those who oppose the death penalty violate the fundamental principle that criminals should be punished according to what they deserve—"making the punishment fit the crime."
  Topic Sentence #2: Also, some people who have lost a loved one to murder believe that they cannot rest until the murderer is executed.
  Topic Sentence #3: The danger of executing an innocent person can hardly be denied by the most ardent proponent of the death penalty, but those who support the death penalty do so because the death penalty, in their view, serves to protect a vastly greater number of innocent lives than are likely to be lost through erroneous application.
                                                                    —Janie Loventhal

Exercise 4: Answer the Professor's Questions

Sometimes, a professor will provide you an essay structure by providing all the questions you need to answer. I suggest a simple outline in this case. On your computer, type in every question separately on its own line. After every question, draw a line under it to help you separate between points.

When you sit down to write, simply give every question at least a full paragraph of an answer. Then, once you have answered it to your satisfaction, scroll down and see what question is next. All you'll need to do is add an introduction, conclusion, transitions, and throw in one point of your own to make yours a little different from everyone else's. See the chapters on development for ideas of how to provide that one unique paragraph.

Exercise 5: Chunking versus Alternating

In argument and research essays, you have many different types of structures to choose from. I'm going to explain two types now, and you can decide if one might work for your essay.

The first type is called chunking. Below is a diagram of that type of essay:

<u>Chunking Model</u>
Introduction
Opposition's Point #1 with Support
Opposition's Point #2 with Support
Opposition's Point #3 with Support
Your Point #1.
(Respond to the opposition's point #1 and then explain your side with support.)
Your Point #2
(Respond to the opposition's point #2 and then explain your side with support.)
Your Point #3
(Respond to the opposition's point #3 and then explain your side with support.)
Conclusion

*As you can see, this type of essay doesn't allow for you to start explaining your side until the end. This "chunking" type works best if all of the points need little explanation and are similar to one another. The next type of structure is called alternating.

<u>Alternating Model</u>
Introduction
Opposition's Point #1 with Support
Your Response to Point #1 with Support and Explanation
Opposition's Point #2 with Support
Your Response to Point #2 with Support and Explanation
And so on. . . .
Conclusion

*This alternating type of essay works best if you have a lot of complex information that is easier to understand if you break it down, point by point.

Pick one of these models and structure your essay. As I mentioned before, there are many types of structures. What is most important is that you know which structure you're using and stay consistent.

Exercise 6: Think as You Write, Write as You Think

Let's say that you refuse to do any sort of outlining and use your first draft as your way to organize your thoughts. That can work as long as you take some time after the first draft and work to organize the second draft. I suggest you buy five different colored highlighters and read the essay once to get a feel for its flow. Then, begin to color-code the different topics. For example, you will color one point in blue, another point in pink, etc. There will be times when you have a stray sentence colored pink that should not be in the blue paragraph. That's your clue that you need to cut and paste some more on the computer. Remember though, if you choose not to outline, you will find that you have some points, maybe great ones, that just don't fit. Be willing to cut them. Most good writers have a big recycle box next to their desks, and they know when to use it.

Exercise 7: Organizing Your Narrative Essays

Narrative essays can appear deceptively easy to organize. Simply, tell your story as it happened. Right? Wrong.

However you write your narrative essay, you must not give equal time to equal time. What I mean by that is do not give the same amount of paragraph space for every hour of your narrative event. Rather, write more about the most meaningful parts of your story and summarize the not-so-meaningful. This point is true no matter how you organize your narrative essay.

For more specific ideas on how to organize your narrative essay, review the three ideas below. Find the idea that would work best for you and design an outline, however rough or simple it may be. I would like to remind you that there are many wonderful ways to organize a narrative, but I have listed below three that work well for my students.

1. CHRONOLOGICAL ORDER
You may want to tell your story in chronological order meaning that you tell the story in the order it happened. First, describe how you were before the event. Then, write about the event itself, and finally, write about how you were after the event.

2. CYCLICAL ORDER

You may also choose to write in a more cyclical fashion. This type of structure would incorporate flashbacks. Or maybe it would begin in the present and move backward in time. I have also seen some successful essays where the writer doesn't tell one story, but a few, distinct events from over a set period of time that are tied together by a common theme that the writer identifies for the reader. While there are many ways to tell a story in cyclical order, make sure you have control over the order and write clear transitions so that the reader understands the leaps in time.

3. STORY BY PICTURES

Find three pictures of yourself that were taken before the story you will write about and then three pictures of yourself that were taken after the story. For each picture, choose one word that describes how you look in the picture. For example, perhaps you see a shy person, an unconfident person, and then you notice a happy person and a proud person.

Once you have your six words, organize the essay so that each paragraph illustrates one of the words from the picture. You do not need to use the word in the paragraph, but simply write the appropriate details and tell the appropriate story that would support that word.

Exercise 8: Open Squares

The following exercise would work well for someone who likes order and visuals. First, determine how many pages your essay should be. Then, decide approximately how many paragraphs the essay will have. Typically, if you are writing a research or argument essay, you will have about two paragraphs per page so that you can have room to incorporate quotes and facts. If you are writing a narrative essay, you might have three paragraphs per page unless of course you plan on using a lot of dialogue.

For each paragraph you plan on writing, draw a large square. The idea now is to write inside each square what that paragraph will discuss. Usually, for every point you plan on making, you will need two paragraphs so that the point can be balanced and well explained. And remember to reserve the first and last squares for the introduction and conclusion.

This exercise can be quite helpful for those writers who try to cram way too many points into one essay.

13
Supporting Evidence

Insufficient detail and abstraction where what is needed is concrete detail, are common—in fact all but universal— in amateur writing. —John Gardner in The Art of Fiction

The power of detail. To a writer, this is the nectar of the gods, the weight of gold, the magic dust of dreams. Without detail, no matter how many hours you work on an essay, the writing will remain lifeless. What's worse, without detail, you cannot support yourself; therefore, you cannot be effective.

We use detail all the time in our casual conversations with friends. It's Saturday at nine a.m., and you cannot wait to call your best friend any longer. "I met the greatest guy last night!" you tell her. Does she begin to enthusiastically squeal and propose a color for the bridesmaid dresses? Of course not. Her first question is, "Who is he? What's he like?" She needs details. She needs details in order to determine if this is the greatest guy ever or if you've picked yet another loser. She needs details to determine what she thinks about him, because not even your best friend will simply accept your opinion. This is important to remember. No friend, no reader, will ever accept your opinion without details for support.

Imagine if you told your best friend this: "Well, he just got out of the Pen and is so attentive. It's like he can't get enough of me. I mean, he's already called five times this morning, and it's only nine o'clock!" These details tell your friend that you need to be advised that this guy isn't a potential husband, but a stalker.

You would provide a different impression if you gave these specifics: "I met him at this church meeting. He's shy, just moved here from Montana, but he got up anyway and played a song on his guitar in front of the entire group although he was so nervous you could see his hands shake. He looks like Brad Pitt, but cuter." Those details provide some endearing facts about him, and your friend might think he *is* the greatest guy and tell you how her complexion looks best in a forest-green bridesmaid dress.

We communicate by details. We persuade by details. We entertain by details.

We do everything by details.

In a research and argument essay, details and facts will mainly support your opinion. For example, if you say the president's environmental policy is harmful, you need to back it up with some facts.

If you are writing a narrative essay, your details will be more scene-oriented and character-based. For example, if you say that you took the worse camping trip ever, mention how no one brought toilet paper and how the baby screamed the entire time because trees scared her.

Now that I have touted the virtues of a good detail, I must say that there are some limitations. To a reader, details signal that this object, this person, this idea, this argument is important. Never provide details just because you have read here that details are good. For example, do not describe a filing cabinet if there isn't something important and crucial in that filing cabinet. Only provide details when what you are saying is important to your overall point.

That being said, welcome to the world of details.

Exercise 1: Show, Don't Tell

"Show, don't tell," is often what I write on a student's essay. For readers, it is much more engaging to have details provided and the judgment left to them to make. For example, instead of writing, "It was a beautiful day," write, "The autumn sky was the color of topaz, and the foliage was as gold as a lady's necklace." The latter example *shows* that the day was pretty, and what's more, it leads the reader to see exactly what the writer wants the reader to see: autumn, sunshine, and optimism.

For example, the following passage is from a student writer who needed to show how hard she worked to make the dance team at school. Notice her use of detail and how she proves that she worked hard without saying that she worked hard:

> *Staying up every night that week with my partners Brianne and Tanya, I made sure that I knew every move to each dance. In hopes that I would get higher kicks and jumps, I put on my five-pound ankle weights each night and did them until I could do them no longer. I wrote down all the steps to each dance and went over them every extra moment that I had throughout my days at school.—Danielle Daunt*

I find that passage to be a good example of how we believe writers more when they show us their points. Someone telling you that she worked hard can come across as an exaggeration until you learn the specific examples behind it.

The following exercise will help you practice showing rather than telling. I have provided a list of "told" statements. Provide details that would show the reader what you want to communicate. Some of the examples are for an argumentative type essay; other examples are for a narrative type essay. Yet, the technique is all the same. Provide details that would show what is being told.

Great Date: _____

Nervous Guy: _____

Tacky Bride: _____

Bad Vacation: _____

Bad Car Wreck: _____

Bad President: _____

Stupid Brother: _____

Environmentally Harmful: _____

Cute Puppy: _____

Racist Speaker: _____

Unhealthy Diet: _____

Low Morale: _____

Exercise 2: Be Specific

One of the techniques professional writers use all the time is choosing a specific word over a general one. For example, trees become Ponderosa pines, birds are starlings, and cats are white Persians. When you use the specific term, you create a clearer, more vivid picture in the reader's mind. Always, the goal with writing is to say exactly what you mean and never anything less. For this exercise, provide a more specific term to the examples provided.

Flower: _____

Dog: _____

Society: _____

Tea: _____

Athlete: _____

Car: _____

Law: _____

Tree: _____

Sickness: _____

Furniture: _____

Exercise 3: Orwell and His Elephant

One of my favorite essays is Orwell's, "Shooting an Elephant." This nonfiction piece is about Orwell's stay in Lower Burma and how he once shot an elephant because the villagers viewed the animal as dangerous. Orwell knew, however, that the elephant eating the long grass in the field was docile as a grandmother. One aspect that all of my classes bring up is how vivid this piece is. Orwell describes the elephant's death never by saying it was agonizing, but instead telling the reader how the blood flowed out of her like red velvet, and how she remained standing bullet after bullet after bullet, only her legs buckling until she finally crumpled down to bleed to death. One of the controversies regarding this essay is that some critics think he made it up yet classified it as non-fiction. In the literary world, this is our version of scandal. My students claim that the narrative must be true because the details are so accurate. Whatever the "right" answer is, my students are correct. The details make the piece seem true, and for a writer, that's all you have to do.

We know details as truth. The better the details, the more we believe the writer, and usually the better we like the essay.

For this exercise, write two short stories about a paragraph long each—one story fake and one story true. Use the best details you can and make them both sound believable. Once you're finished, read your stories to a class and have everyone guess which is accurate. The goal here is to fool everyone. Put realistic details in that fake scene as if it were as well known to you as your own home.

Exercise 4: A Picture Tells a Thousand Stories

This exercise works best for a classroom environment. Everyone should bring in a picture of a person who is a stranger to the class. Without saying a word about the person in the picture, exchange photos with someone in your class. Each of you will then write a description about the stranger's life based upon the details that you can see in the picture. Here are a few questions that you can answer:

What is the person's name?

What is this person's big dream?

What does the person fear the most?

What is the person's personality like?

What is the person's most annoying habit?

What is the love status?

What is difficult about this exercise is that you must provide details from the picture that support your judgments, whatever they may be. If you say the person is outgoing, you must explain what is in the picture, in specific terms, that gives you that idea. For example, if you want to say that the person in the picture is fun-loving or a jokester, support that judgment with facts from the picture. Perhaps you can say this because the guy is playing the drums, is closing his eyes, and has the other people around him laughing. The reason behind this exercise is simple: as writers, we must be able to give details that will make the readers infer our intended conclusions.

When you finish writing, read to each other what life you have given the person in the picture. When I have done this exercise before in class, the results were frighteningly accurate. Students have correctly named the characters, correctly given the professions, and correctly analyzed their strengths and weaknesses.

Exercise 5: From the Bottom, Up

When you begin to describe something, you need to describe it according to a specific order. Imagine that your eyes are a movie camera, and you want to describe your parents' home. Say you begin filming as you go up the brick walk. What you first see is the outside of the house with its oversized columns in a middle class neighborhood, and then you see the front door with a big gaudy wreath. The door opens into a foyer where both your parents stand, hovering and smiling, until finally you are moving inside the house and enter the dining room with the table filled with bowls of steaming peas and potatoes. The point here is that when you decide to describe something, you must follow a logical order of how one would view it. For example, begin on the outside of the house and move in to the dining room table. This structure is going from the large picture to the small picture. You can also begin small, with the pictures on the fridge and then move outside to describe a brick two-story home. When you describe a person, the structure should again follow some order. Begin at the head and move down to the feet for example.

Pick one of the following objects (your car, your home, your best friend) to describe and decide on a structure in which to describe it: large to small, small to large, top to bottom, bottom to top, outside to inside, or inside to outside. Now, start filming with your eyes and show us what to see in the order you have chosen.

Exercise 6: I Saw Not

We often write "I noticed," "I looked at," or "I saw" in our essays. These expressions are pointless because your name on the piece of writing indicates that your eyes did the seeing. Delete those words and simply tell us what you saw.

Exercise 7: Add 'Em In

Go through your essay and circle whenever you tell rather than show. Then, pick three of the most important areas where you need to add details to show your point and do it.

Student Sample: (Notice how the second sentence supports the first sentence with a fact.)

Making money by being a musician is difficult. The Rolling Stones made more money off of t-shirts and bandanas from their 1995 Voo-doo Lounge tour than they did by ticket sales.

—Will Owen

14
Introductions

*The pages are still blank, but there is a miraculous feeling
of the words being there, written in invisible ink
and clamoring to become visible. —Vladimir Nabokov*

Writing the first sentence of an essay can often be the single, most difficult sentence in the entire piece of writing. (And subsequently, the most procrastinated sentence.) Some writers feel that sentence carries a lot of weight because it is the first one read. That fact, however, shouldn't put you into a frenzy, hijacking all of your time with the idea that the sentence must be perfect before you can go on. These writers who seek perfection with their first sentences often have nothing to show but pink eraser dust. Other writers are anxious about their topic and look to the first sentence as if it is a sign from above forecasting if they should abort the essay topic or celebrate it. Most writers, though, agonize over that first sentence because this is the point where perception meets reality. Simply put, you get to find out if your idea is as good as you think it is. One student who never felt as if his end product was as good as what he had imagined it would be, turned in an essay with only one word typed on the page: "Ruined."

One can take comfort that every writer faces this problem, and obviously, many writers, if not all, have worked through it. I'm not saying it will be easy. Most of my students tell me they spend more time rewriting that first paragraph than any other. But since so many writers before us have encountered the same problem, there are quite a few tricks to help get your writing started and grab the reader's attention. I want to stress that before you start writing your introduction, it is ideal to have already done some prewriting exercises from the earlier section. One final point here is that this chapter does not delve into the thesis statement that will ideally come at the end of your introduction paragraph. For more help on writing that thesis statement, see chapter ten. What we have in this chapter are techniques to get everything started.

Exercise 1: Why This Topic?

Every essay, every poem, every story has what many professional writers call a kernel or a germ. A kernel is that moment of inspiration when you get the idea for your essay. To an outsider, this moment can seem as useless as a broken cup. To you, it is the genesis of it all. For this exercise, write down what gave you the idea to do your particular essay topic. Some act a friend did, something you heard, something you saw had to trigger the idea in your mind. Did a segment on the news frustrate you? A conversation with a friend? For example, if it was a conversation with a friend, write that down, in detail. Describe the room, the music, perhaps the argument, whatever it was that inspired you. If it was simply a memory, what triggered that memory? Even if you were assigned an essay topic, what single event caused you to come to your particular response? And I must say, beginning an essay with a truthful confession such as you didn't understand a particular sonnet by Shakespeare or you never had a firm opinion on the death penalty is a solid route to beginning an essay. Write it all down! This type of introduction will grab the reader's attention because the reader will understand why the topic has relevance in your life. So, right now, write down what brought you to your essay topic.

Exercise 2: It Was a Dark and Stormy Night . . . .

There is a reason why Snoopy begins his novels with this sentence; it immediately starts the work off with action that draws the reader into your essay. For this introduction technique, take your topic, for example gun control, and begin your essay with a little story that would relate to your essay and start it off with action. For example, you can begin by having your dad stomp down to the basement on a cold, fall morning before his hunt to retrieve the rifle from the gun safe. Don't worry about introducing the anecdote or explaining what you're doing. Later you can say how the anecdote relates to your essay topic with a sentence or two. Right now, simply tell a story, fiction or fact, that relates to your essay. This way, like Snoopy, you are beginning your essay with action.

Student Sample:
  Emma and her husband, Dan, have young children. Their family decides to go out for pizza one evening. When they arrive at the restaurant, the only section available without having to wait is smoking. Their children are cranky because they are hungry, and the wait is at least twenty minutes. Emma and Dan both know their children will not be able to wait that long. So they accept the table in the smoking section. As Emma and her family

follow the hostess to the table, she is suffocated by the odor. She has never been fond of the smell, but many friends and family smoke, so she has always just tolerated it. But why should her innocent children have to be put through that or anyone else for that matter?

—Brianne Wells

Exercise 3: Beginning with the End

Many good writers know that the best way to tell a story is often not to begin at the beginning. For this exercise, write the conclusion first. Don't even worry about the introduction and write what you imagine you would say at the end of your essay. I especially recommend doing this exercise if you have a lot of perfectionist tendencies that might actually impede your progress. Or, if you would prefer, forget about the introduction and start writing the second paragraph. Once you start writing, you warm up and can better approach a more challenging paragraph like the introduction later.

Exercise 4: The Outsider Speaks

Although we all have different voices we project on the page, most student writers strive to have their writing sound reasonable and intelligent. One way to help achieve this goal is to dedicate the opening paragraph to the opposition's point of view. How this introduction will work is you will first give four to five sentences explaining the opposition's case to your topic, and then you will simply say that you do not share that view. All you have to do is provide your thesis at the end. (Check out "The Although Clause" thesis exercise in chapter ten on how to do this.) For now, try to write the paragraph from the point of view of somebody who would disagree with what you have to say and provide their rationale. Do this with respect which means give their best points and write this introduction as convincingly and honestly as you can.

Exercise 5: Frame

This is one of my favorite techniques for it solves what to do with your introduction and your conclusion, a bargain in writing tricks. The basic premise here is that you need to think of a short story (an anecdote) that showcases your topic. For example, if you are writing about the benefits of living together before marriage, you could begin the essay with a guy unpacking boxes at his new place and wondering as he's putting up her bright, daisy dishes if this is the right decision. Then, in the final paragraph, finish your story. This is the frame. Let us know what happened to that guy who was unpacking her daisy-themed dinnerware with matching napkins. Since your thesis is for living together, you want to end the story on a positive note. If your thesis was against living together before marriage, you could show him regretting the decision and moving out as a result of a break-up. Think now about your topic and write down three possible scenarios that would effectively frame your essay. Choose the best one and begin writing the story. Use the first part of the story for the introduction.

> *Student Sample:*
>   First Paragraph: *She sits in her room on a chenille pillow she made herself, surrounded by collected articles, looking through Martha Stewart's Living, House Beautiful, and other home decor magazines for inspiration. She does not own a house; she has not even entered college, yet she collects these articles much like a girl her age would be collecting make-up tips from Seventeen or Marie Claire. She is full of creative ideas for her house that she will one day own and for the curtains that she will one day sew for it.*
>   Concluding Paragraph: *The girl, now in college, is aware that there are options for someone wanting a creative outlet in a stable and personally satisfying career. She still has not fully decided as to what she wants to do in just a few short years from now, but she is aware of what to look for in a career. She plans on putting to use all of the do-it-yourself and design books she has read and all of the inventive ideas she has been harboring. The girl, like her pattern for her curtains, is ready to cut along the dotted line of education in order to pin the guide onto the fabric to create the tapestry of her life.*
>
>   —Shelby Thurman

Exercise 6: Meat and Potatoes

For this introduction, the writer gets straight to the point. In this exercise, write in the first paragraph what you plan to say, why it needs to be said (the relevance it has to class and/or life), and how you'll say it (meaning the structure the essay will have). If you are comfortable writing a thesis, do that, too. Then, you are done with the introduction and can move on to dessert.

15
Development

Why are we reading if not in hope that the writer will magnify and dramatize our days, will illuminate and inspire us with wisdom and courage and the possibility of meaningfulness and will press upon our minds the deepest mysteries so we may feel again their majesty and power. —Annie Dillard from The Writing Life

I have a confession to make; sometimes the essays that earn an "A" have earned the "A" not because of what I have taught them, but because of something special within the essay. I slowly realize as I sit at my kitchen table with a steaming cup of coffee in front of me that the essay I'm grading is good, is great, is better than what I could have done at that student's age. And why is that? Talent? No, not talent.

An essay stands out because of its complexity, its development. Often, a professor will write on your essay that you need more development, but what does that mean exactly? Good development means that your essay provides complex, critical thinking to a subject. Essentially, your writing shows that you reflected, questioned, and reflected some more, creating insights that made my day a little more interesting.

Good development is moving the essay past the typical and expected and having the essay bring about real questions and insights into the topic. It is about being the opposite of simple and predictable, traits that some young writers claim that they just cannot help. As Annie Dillard stated in the epigraph above, writing should "illuminate and inspire us with wisdom and courage and the possibility of meaningfulness." The student essays that I remember have brought that element of wisdom, courage, and meaningfulness to the reader. The relationship between purposeful, explorative thinking and the resulting original insight is what readers long for in an essay.

I would like to add that good development is not your B.S. section. What you need to remember is why one writes and why one reads. People read to be entertained, to be educated, to be taught something. If I'm bored while reading your essay because the essay repeats the same points we've all heard, then the essay is not doing its job and keeping its commitment to the reader to be worth his time. In an essay, you must say something new.

65

While it is easy to recognize good, complex development, it is much more difficult to learn how to do it. I do not believe that simplistic essays are representative of a simplistic mind. Rather, good developmental skills can be learned. They must be learned. But more importantly, as writers we must understand good development is necessary to a successful essay and be willing to do the tough work. So, how do you develop your essay? Try a few of the exercises below and see what works for you. Also, once you have a first draft completed, check out the advanced development chapter in the revising section.

Exercise 1: Targeted Freewrites

1. Question yourself! With your thesis in mind, ask yourself when might your thesis be incorrect? In other words, in what situations and circumstances might your argument not work? Also, when are you especially right? As you do this freewrite, record everything that you are thinking, including the minor points and the contradictions. Don't skip ahead of your own self, but write everything down.

2. Do a freewrite on what you don't know concerning your topic. Once you finish the freewrite, add one of these points to your essay and talk it out. Remember, someone who is completely confident and never doubts his opinions is someone who is either bluffing or simple-minded. Intelligent writing identifies exceptions, flaws, and points of ignorance in one's own logic. Granted, there is a fine balance here. You don't want to write an essay listing only questions and saying how you don't know anything. But the reader does appreciate a little dose of humility and honesty in an essay. For example, if you are writing an essay on taxes, admit how even experienced economists claim they sometimes do not know what will work best for the economy until they see the practical results of their ideas.

Exercise 2: When in Doubt, Classify

One of the best ways to bring in complexity is to identify the "gray areas" to your topic. A gray area would be a point or example that does not have a clear right or wrong answer. To help you discuss these areas, try classification. Classification is when you break down a larger issue into different classifications or types. When you classify, be sure to explain the subtle differences in each group. This will encourage you to discuss distinctions which is also a good technique to help add development. To help you better understand how to use classification for your essay, follow the exercise below.

PART A

First, practice classification. Classify the freshmen at your school into six or more different groups, giving each group a creative name. Then, provide a description for each group being sure to include a list of distinctions that makes that particular student group different from other groups.

PART B

What is the main topic your essay is discussing. Friendships? Punishments? Human Rights? Try the classification exercise again, this time classifying your main topic into different categories.

Exercise 3: Throw Out Webster's!

One of the best techniques to add complexity to your essay is to define your key terms. A key term is any word that you use repeatedly in your essay. What you need to do is to define your key term according to what it means to you. To define it exactly, you will need to also ask yourself how it differs from most people's definition of the word. For example, if you are writing an essay on animal rights, take a few sentences to define "rights." Are rights guaranteed in your opinion to all creatures? What would basic rights for animals be?

The reason why it is wise to define your key terms is because many of our nation's debates are actually debates over the definition of a word such as "abortion." At the center of this debate is the issue of when life begins. One side might contend that life begins at conception while the other side might say at birth.

For this exercise, decide what are/is your key term(s). Define this for your reader in your second paragraph. And remember, stay away from Webster's Dictionary. What your essay needs is your unique definition of your key terms that will reveal the crux of your debates. Define your key terms in a way that establishes the foundation for your essay's discussion.

> *Student Sample: (Notice how the student defines the term "impact.")*
> *What I have always wanted to do and still want to do is impact jazz music. This impact would be in the truest sense of the word. I want to help in developing jazz into something new and unique while honoring all the wonderful music that has come before me.*
> *—Clayton Rothwell*

Exercise 4: Story Time

We never grow old of a good story. One way to keep your essay interesting is to provide a personal anecdote. I have mentioned this technique a few times in the book because it is so useful in curing many writing problems, an essay panacea. What a personal anecdote does is provide a moment of relief from the logical reasoning. You write a short story, no more than one paragraph, about yourself or maybe someone else that is relevant to your essay. And, yes, these personal anecdotes are completely acceptable in a formal essay, even in biology essays.

For this exercise, find one place, typically near the end of the essay or the very beginning, where you can insert a personal anecdote. Then, do it.

Student Sample:

I've got a confession to make: when I said earlier that I never thought about work at all until I was a sophomore, I was lying. There were times before I got involved with music, before thoughts of music business even existed, when I was forced to talk of careers. In middle school job survey tests, when aunts are drilling for answers to all the typical questions that aunts usually ask—in any of these situations I'd spit out the same rehearsed answer with no meaning behind it: "I could see myself in advertising." The main reason for that 6th grade response was that I imagined advertising to be a mix of creativity and business, and that sounded fun.

—Chris Rorie

Exercise 5: One Moment in Time

One of the great joys I find in reading student essays is that I often learn something new. I come away feeling refreshed—and liking the essay better. One technique that helps guarantee that your reader will learn something new is to provide historical evidence.

To provide historical evidence, briefly research the history of your topic and write a few sentences about it. You can do this for a variety of topics such as the death penalty, taxes, the Internet, purses, etc. The answers are often fascinating and provide a strong start to your essay.

Another use of historical evidence is to find a similar case in history regarding your topic and make a comparison. For example, a student's essay on legalizing marijuana may want to provide a paragraph on the effects of the 1920s alcohol prohibition. Surprisingly, many of the effects of banning alcohol are similar to the effects of banning marijuana today. Or, if you were writing a narrative on your parents' divorce, you could add some historical information on divorce for added interest and depth.

Historical evidence shows real life applications and is therefore quite convincing. Also, if you're dealing with an emotional debate, taking a step back in time helps to calm down both sides by offering some perspective. Although providing historical evidence may only take fifteen minutes of your time, the result is worth it. For this exercise, provide at least one example of historical evidence in your essay.

16
More on Addressing the Opposition

In the prewriting section, I discussed the importance of addressing the opposition. For argument and research essays, you will need to work more on this technique and the following exercises should provide you with what you need to add.

To address the opposition, you need to have an idea of what the other side is thinking and feeling—and state it. When you discuss a tense topic with a friend, you know exactly what will make her vow never to speak to you again, and you also know, or have an idea, where you can find common ground. You know this by instinct and common sense. This same instinct and common sense has to be applied to your essay.

For more advanced work on addressing the opposition, complete the following exercises. If the concept of addressing the opposition is new to you, refer to chapter eleven.

Exercise 1: Playing Devil's Advocate

This exercise requires a classroom to work best. Here, the instructor will have a stop watch or egg timer and instruct everyone in the room to pair up. The point is to play devil's advocate with each other. Tell your topic to your partner and have your partner pretend to be the opposition. The "opposition" will then provide logical support for his/her ideas. When you have finished discussing your topic, ask your partner his topic and then you get to play devil's advocate. When the timer dings, quickly find another person and do it again. (I suggest taking notes the entire time.) Once you are finished with the dialogue, sit down and write for ten minutes on the best points you heard for the opposition. The goal is to find some excellent opposition for your essay.

Exercise 2: A (Little) Admission of Defeat

Sometimes you are going to get tripped up when you argue. You write something from the opposition's standpoint, and gasp, you believe it. How do you get out of that? The solution that immediately comes to most student writers is to lie. Who would know after all? Never, and I repeat, never lie in your essay. The truth is always more interesting.

When you hit this roadblock, concede. Admit that you agree with the opposition's viewpoint on this small point. But explain, to the reader and to yourself, how you can agree to that one small point but disagree concerning the larger issue.

A concession can also defuse the skeptical reader who might use one small objection to discard your entire argument. If you can defuse this small objection by conceding, you may persuade your opposition.

Whenever students have conceded a point or two in the past, I've been completely impressed with their maturity and insight.

Exercise 3: Visualizing the Enemy

Students tell me that they do their best work when they can picture an actual person who disagrees with them. For this exercise, try to think of someone—a friend, a boss, a sibling—who does not share your viewpoint. Write the essay directed at that person. One successful example that comes to my mind is a young woman who had worked a full-time job a few years before she returned to school. She felt as if our traditional forty-hour work week was too long and wanted to write an essay about reducing the work week to thirty-five hours. Throughout her research, she visualized what her boss would have said to each of her ideas. In the end, she wrote a convincing essay on how one could actually be more productive working less hours.

For this exercise, visualize a specific person who would oppose your position and work to persuade that person.

Exercise 4: Show Respect

In addressing the opposition, it is crucial that you always show respect toward the other side. If you insult the opposition, imply stupidity or immorality in any way, it reflects negatively on you. The reason is the same as it was on the playground in first grade: you must pick on someone your own size. If you show disrespect toward someone in your essay, that person has no way to defend himself which makes you look like a belligerent bully.

For this exercise, go through your essay and analyze your tone and language. Any time you think you are becoming a bit shrill, combative, or rude, change it.

17
Conclusions

A strange, green-furred beast roams through high schools. It is has five heads and smothers you to death and is known by the name The Five Paragraph Essay. Now, I don't want to discredit this form too much because the form does help teach you how to write. But kill the beast when you enter college. Essay assignments in college won't typically be limited to one question that requires three paragraphs to support your position and one paragraph of introduction along with a concluding paragraph that says what you have just said. In college, your ideas should be too complex and too developed to fit comfortably into that form.

Of all the drawbacks to The Five Paragraph Essay, the one that I dislike the most is the concluding paragraph. The conclusion idea in The Five Paragraph Essay is to restate what you've said and summarize your thesis. Here's the deal. I can remember what you have said in a two-page essay. Senility hasn't hit me yet. And since I remember what you said, repeating the information means that you are being repetitive which means I am bored which means I'm bored on the last paragraph right before I determine your grade. Do you see the five-car pile up in motion?

To write a good conclusion, you need to ask yourself what is the purpose of the final paragraph. Either you have persuaded the reader by the last paragraph or you haven't. This is the first point that needs to sink in. There is nothing you can say that will persuade the reader in the last five sentences that the previous hundred and five sentences have not been able to do. So, if the point of the conclusion isn't to persuade and convince, what should it do?

Several things. For one, the paragraph should provide a sense of finality and have one sentence that summarizes the essay. But what should the bulk of the last paragraph do? Think of this paragraph as the emotional reinforcement paragraph. The reader has read the last few pages, which were logical, and now it is time to bring in the emotion. Essentially, seal the deal, if I may use a business term, with an emotional, good-feeling, last paragraph.

Below are a few options that will help you finish your essay. Try a few and see which one works best. Also, do remember to provide a summary of your essay, but just do it in one, effective sentence.

Exercise 1: Let It Sit

The best suggestion I can offer you regarding your conclusion is inspired from a cooking technique. If you have ever watched anyone bake bread from scratch, there is always that moment of rest that the dough requires in order to rise fully. Writing works the same way. If you've been writing your essay for a while, do not blaze through and write that conclusion in the same sitting as the rest of the essay. I can tell every time my students do that because the last paragraph takes on an obligatory, dull feeling, that I'm-almost-outta-here vibe. Instead, wait one day if you can before you write the conclusion. If you can't do that, at least go do something else and then come back to your essay after thirty minutes. Reread the essay and see what you have yet to say that needs to be mentioned.

Exercise 2: Call to Action

The call to action technique is a great one for a typical argument/research type of essay. In this technique, you tell the reader what to do that would help support your thesis. For example, let's say that you have been talking about the negative effects of not exercising. What you would do for this type of conclusion is provide the reader with some ideas of what he/she could do to start exercising. For example, find the school's gym rate and say, "For only ten dollars a month, a student, staff, or faculty member can enroll in an exercise program and have full access to nautilus equipment, free weights, and an indoor track, which is especially appealing in cold weather." Perhaps your essay was more political in nature. Your call to action could be asking the reader to write his/her congressperson. The idea here is to rally your troops without being preachy, so write this last paragraph with a lot of energy and positive enthusiasm—and tell your readers what to do.

Exercise 3: Frame

This is the same technique that is mentioned in the chapter on introductions. With the frame technique, you have a solution for both the introduction and the conclusion paragraphs. My grandmother would call this thrifty.

The basic premise here is that you need to think of a short story (an anecdote) that showcases your topic. If the essay is against the words "under God" in the Pledge of Allegiance, you would think of a story that could relate to that issue. In the introduction paragraph, you begin the story, and in the conclusion, you conclude it. For example, in the first paragraph you could show a class of fifth graders rising to say the pledge, all except one little boy. Then, in the conclusion, you could show the other kids harassing that one child in the cafeteria because he didn't say the pledge. This is the frame and serves as a way to tie the essay together.

Exercise 4: Heightened Language

This technique is one of my favorites. All throughout your essay, you have been writing logically and scientifically. The conclusion is your time to cut loose. Use metaphors, abstract images, vivid details and as much emotion as you wish. Martin Luther King, Jr. did this beautifully in *Letter from Birmingham Jail*. Here is the last sentence of his essay: "Let us all hope that the dark clouds of racial prejudice will soon pass away and the deep fog of misunderstanding will be lifted from our fear-drenched communities and in some not too distant tomorrow the radiant stars of love and brotherhood will shine over our great nation with all of their scintillating beauty."

Look at all of the abstract images in that line: "dark clouds of racial prejudice," "deep fog of misunderstanding," and "radiant stars of love and brotherhood." If this sentence opened the essay, the reader would wonder what was going on, but as a concluding sentence, the reader welcomes the artistic nature of the line because it's different and appeals to them on an emotional and visual level.

For this type of conclusion paragraph, use heightened language which means metaphors, poetic images, abstract language, and a good dose of passion.

Exercise 5: Personal Anecdote

For this exercise, tell a personal story about yourself that relates to the essay topic. Let the reader understand your personal connection to this essay.

Student Sample (From an essay on the benefits of coal):
As you have read this paper, you might have wondered what besides the evident facts have made my conclusion, and I would like to explain them so that you have a better understanding of my position. As a child, I grew up in Southern Illinois, outside of a town of about 5,000 people. However, my hometown had once been the center for coal production in the region. Nearly eighty years ago the town was a city of about 22,000, which supported eight coal mines surrounding the city. It was because of this that my great grandparents settled there. My family is full of people who made their living working in underground coal mines, including my great uncle who after 50 years working in the mines was named Old King Coal. Furthermore, my dad has made his living working in the industry. After years of mining, he made the leap to coal sales and is now the Vice President of the largest mining company in the Midwest, which is a division of the largest mining company in the world. It is due to this history that I understand the power of coal and its usefulness in a day where life as we know it would be impossible.

—Brett Galli

Exercise 6: Quote

A quote from a new source often provides a strong sense of finality and allows someone else the struggle of finding a good last sentence. All you have to do is find a good quote. Check out *Bartlett's Familiar Quotations* or look up quotes on the Web.

Exercise 7: Take It to the Universe

Whenever I get a poem published, I try to give my mother a copy of it. If she loves it, she'll put it in her guest bathroom. At first, I was insulted. The bathroom? Not a poetic place to say the least. Then, I realized what she was doing. She thought that those poems in her bathroom would have a universal appeal. Someone, free of the bias of a mother's love, could also enjoy the poems. The truth is, my goal now is to make it to my mother's guest bathroom because this means that she thinks my poems have a universal appeal.

Let me provide an example of an essay with universal appeal. Let's say that your essay had been talking about your family's high rate of breast cancer. You mainly focused on what a woman could do to reduce her odds of getting the disease. All of this is fine, but if the reader doesn't have a family history of breast cancer, the reader may not quite care about the topic. In the last paragraph, find something more universal than the issue of breast cancer. Attach it to women's health in general or new discoveries in the field such as the idea that cancer may be a virus.

For this conclusion technique, have the last paragraph offer a universal element. To write this, ask yourself what topic could you link to your essay that is in some way bigger than your essay topic? Or ask yourself to find the element within your topic that all readers could relate to. Find the universal element and explore it for your conclusion.

Exercise 8: Provide Solutions

A positive ending is always better than a negative one due to the fact that the reader would prefer to end the essay feeling optimistic about the world. Yet, you don't want to be Pollyannish about it, providing an overly simplistic solution that requires everyone to hold hands in an effort to end all wars. What works well is to provide real, honest solutions to whatever problems your essay has discussed. The solutions should complete the essay, and also make the reader feel as if a better society is in the near future.

Student Sample:

   Cooking offers a great variety of benefits to those who know its methods. Cooking meals not only provides the body with the vitamins and nutrients it needs to survive, but it unites all people together as they sit down to eat a meal. To insure the health and unity of people throughout America, make cooking a part of general education in school for children. Give all children the opportunity to learn ways to be self-sufficient in their meals. Provide all people the opportunity to know the options cooking provides for their life, health, friends and family, and their future.

—Jennifer B. Moss

18
Titles

Writing a title may be what you create last, yet a title is what the reader sees first. Therefore, the title is the first element of your work that a reader judges. Titles, however, are rarely given much thought by student writers mainly because of lack of time. If there is a title, it is often dry and dull and lifted directly from the assignment sheet such as *Argument Essay Number One*. Most of the time, there is no title at all. I once heard a poet say that having an untitled piece of writing is like having an unnamed child—I have to agree. In fiction writing, everyone knows the importance of a title. That is why writers have "working titles." Working titles allow writers the freedom to change the title at the last minute because a title must be exactly right. It should capture one's attention and provide some summary of the writing.

A few people have a knack for titles, but most of us have to try a few of them to see what works. F Scott Fitzgerald's *The Great Gatsby* was first titled *Hurrah for the Red, White and Blue*. How bad is that? *The Sun Also Rises* by Hemingway was first coined *Fiesta*.

To create a title that will provide a good first impression, try the following exercises.

Exercise 1: Thievery Strikes Again

T.S. Eliot once said, "Amateurs borrow, professionals steal." He didn't mean that one should plagiarize, but the quote does imply that one needs to study and copy great writers' techniques in order to improve one's craft. This is one of the reasons why art students first paint copies of masterpieces; they need to understand what the greats were doing—and then emulate them.

For this exercise, I want you to look at your English book and pick three intriguing titles. If you don't have an English text, grab a book that features a variety of essays from many writers such as a collection of the best essays from the previous year. It doesn't matter if you've never read the essays. Simply pick three favorite titles from the table of contents. My favorite ones from my class's anthology are "Reflections on a Lettuce Wedge," "Why Boys Don't Play with Dolls," and "The Clan of One-Breasted Women."

Next, figure out why you like the ones that you like. What is it exactly that makes it work? If you come up with an answer like "it sounds cool," try again. Be specific so that you can imitate the writer's technique. Later, you will apply the same technique to your essay and invent a title. For example, "Reflections on a Lettuce Wedge" interests me because it is so serious about something that is quite unphilosophical—a lettuce wedge. I'm intrigued to see what sort of profound reflection one could have regarding iceberg lettuce. I like "Why Boys Don't Play with Dolls" because it sounds confident and answers a question that society has posed. "The Clan of One-Breasted Women" grabs my attention by using a word unique to a literary essay, "breast," and because I don't quite know what it means until I read the essay.

Once you figure out why you like the titles, write copies of them. To "copy" in writing, use the same technique, construction, or structure as the professional writer. For example, if I copied the titles I mentioned previously, I would title my book "Reflections on Pink Eraser Dust" or "Why Students Don't Write Well." Relate your imitations to your essay topic and see what happens.

Exercise 2: Lead with a Question

Many great discoveries were first unanswered questions. For an interesting title, a question can serve as a solid title like Judy Blume's *Are You There, God? It's Me, Margaret*. For this exercise, think of a question that your essay actually answers and have that be the title. Come up with three possible questions as titles.

Exercise 3: Using Allusions

Some titles everyone remembers although they may never have read the book or seen the movie. For example, *Gone with the Wind*, *For Whom the Bell Tolls*, and *Star Wars* are all titles that the majority of Americans know.

For interesting titles, you can use cultural and literary allusions. Think of some of your favorite titles and play with their wording so that the titles reflect your essay topic. For instance, if I were using a literary allusion to title this book, I would title it *For Whom the Essay Tolls*. Referencing a well known work establishes a link between your essay and the culture at large.

19
Paragraphs

Paragraphs.

Some writers know exactly when to hit that tab key and move on to the next paragraph. Like a sax player in a jazz band, this writer knows when to end the solo.

Other writers feel as if their essay is a marathon and their fingers must keep moving until the end. Breaks, such as paragraphs and going to the bathroom, are to be dealt with later. Better yet, paragraph breaks are for the professor or another reader to figure out.

How to form your paragraphs is simple and complex. One begins a new paragraph when one begins a new thought. I didn't say an entirely different topic, but a new thought. In an essay, everything will relate, or it should, so it can be difficult to understand when exactly that new idea occurs. One suggestion I have is to pay attention to your own reactions. When you slap hard on the period button, that often signals you are done with the paragraph. When you feel excited about another idea, often you need a new paragraph there. Aside from your own instincts, look at the page itself and see if you have a big block of black ink. Rarely is that necessary.

Some people may say that they love long paragraphs. After all, many great writers such as Faulkner are known to have paragraphs as long as the Nile. Readers, however, prefer short to medium-sized paragraphs. It is easier on the eyes and easier to review what you have said. Imagine a newspaper with no paragraphs but only black blocks of words. Would you read that sipping your coffee as you try to wake up?

I have provided an outline for the classic type of paragraph structure. If you feel as if you know how to form paragraphs naturally, then move on. But if you would like a refresher course, take advantage of this moment.

Overall Structure of the Paragraph

1. Topic sentence

The topic sentence, which is the first sentence of a paragraph, presents the paragraph's subject. You must have this. Think of it as your thesis statement for the paragraph. Also, the topic sentence must contain some type of transition from the previous paragraph. The rest of the sentences relate in one of the following ways to the topic sentence:

2. Explain the topic sentence.

3. Support the topic sentence.
In a research essay, this is where you quote and discuss your outside sources. Never end the paragraph with quoted material.

4. Conclude the paragraph.
I find that this is the sentence that students omit the most, but a paragraph needs a sense of finality just as the essay needs that sense, too. Note: The concluding sentence either transitions into the next paragraph or concludes the paragraph's discussion.

Exercise 1: Pick a Point

Pick one point that your essay will discuss and write a paragraph in the classic structure that I have provided above. Pay close attention to how every sentence leads into the next one and reflects the topic sentence.

Exercise 2: Division

Paragraphs can help you organize your essay. Take advantage of this fact and write a rough outline of what each paragraph will talk about. Write the paragraph's topic in one sentence only. (Forcing yourself to summarize your paragraph in one sentence will help define each paragraph.) Once you have your paragraph outline, start writing your essay, one paragraph at a time. Remember, those who write good essays, first write good paragraphs.

20
Audience

Sometimes students will complain how one professor wants a certain writing style, but their high school teacher had told them that style was incorrect. The longer they take college courses, the more writing contradictions they learn. For example, as juniors they might tell me that a professor in the biology department demanded no quotes while their English professors stressed the use of quotes to support opinions. Students will often tell these tales with their arms crossed and their chins jutting forward as if these contradictions are signs that no one truly knows how to write well—and professors just pretend like they know.

Not so. Realizing that educated people have different ideas concerning good writing is the beginning of the realization that one must write for one's audience. Rather than feel flustered that you are expected to write in different ways for different circumstances, feel proud that you are learning how to write in a variety of forms. From high school, to college, to the work place, your writing will be faced with different demands, and the good writer understands meeting those demands is called writing to one's audience.

Since writing's primary goal is to communicate, adapting to your audience (or to your professor's criteria) is part of the process. In everything you write, you must determine who is your audience and what is the best way to write for that audience. For example, I wrote this book in a tone and style different from that of an essay I wrote for fellow professors. As a writer, you need to know what you want to say and then write what you want to say in a way that best fits your intended audience.

Exercise 1: Who Are You Talking To?

Answer the following questions to help determine your audience and therefore your writing's style, form, and tone.

1. Who is my audience?

_____

_____

2. What is the quality of writing they expect to receive?

   _____

   _____

3. How formal should my language be? For example, will I use contractions, slang, and/or first person?

   _____

   _____

4. How can I give my audience a product better than what they expect, but still within the expected parameters?

   _____

   _____

5. What will be my most persuasive points for this audience?

   _____

   _____

6. What points should I exclude for this audience?

   _____

   _____

7. What does this audience already know?

   _____

   _____

8. What would they like to know?

   _____

   _____

9. What do they need to know?

   _____

   _____

10. What does this audience need so that they feel the writing was worthwhile to read?

    _____

    _____

Exercise 2: Take Back the Power

Every semester, I discuss with my students the power a typical reader possesses and the power a typical writer possesses. We limit our conversation to non-fiction writing since that is the majority of what we write in college.

First, we list all the different examples of non-fiction writing that we can imagine: book reviews, science articles, obituaries, editorials, autobiographies, biographies, news articles, memoirs, and medical announcements. Then, we begin the discussion of who has the majority of the power. Usually, it is the writer who has the most power because he/she writes to persuade, to inform, to entertain, and to call others to act. The reader can choose to respond or not respond, but the majority of the reader's actions are passive. For example, they read to be entertained, to be informed, to be compelled to act. For example, when reading a book review, the reader may choose not to buy the book, but the writer has the majority of the power because it is the writer's opinion that influences many readers' opinions.

This power equation remains true for most forms of non-fiction until one examines the student essay. Here, the traditional power structure is reversed. The reader of the student essay, which is the professor, has the power to grade, to critique, and to teach one how to write. The writer is in the weaker position because he is being forced to write and is usually being taught how to write or being taught a particular subject.

Since the power structure is distorted with student essays, it is not surprising that some student writers hate to write for classes whereas they love to write outside of school. After all, writing without power is unnatural.

What is the solution? If you are writing an essay where your reader will be the one with the majority of power, try to add elements that help you regain that power. Write a freewrite on each of the following questions to see what you can add to your essay that will help equalize the power structure.

1. What could you include in your essay (or use as a topic even) that your professor has not experienced personally, but you have? For example, one student whose biology professor required her to write on the harmful effects of tanning beds, specifically on the cancerous effects, chose to write about the people whom she met because her father was a doctor who treated patients with cancer. Every summer, her entire family would attend a camp for people recovering from cancer. Her essay focused on what the biology professor wanted, which was a scientific explanation of how cancer forms, but the writer also included one paragraph about the trials of fighting cancer that she had witnessed.

2. What aspect of the essay do you care about passionately? Even though professors often assign topics, the topics can reveal many different answers. Choose the path that you care about the most.

Exercise 3: Them's Fighting Words

Some words are so loaded with negative connotations they may be as disastrous as a truck loaded with dynamite sitting outside a city park. In your writing, you want to take the time to make sure no phrases or words will distract your audience from your overall message. The following exercise is not an exercise in being politically correct, but rather an exercise to ensure that you don't needlessly upset a reader and in the end, derail your argument.

1. What unstated assumptions might you have toward your reader? For example, do you believe your reader to be ignorant on your chosen topic or well educated? How religious did you view your reader, how political, how well read, etc.?

_____

_____

2. How can you address those unstated assumptions in the essay?

_____

_____

3. Do you have any language that needs to be deleted that implies disapproval to the other side and/or that develops an "us versus them" mentality? Check your essay to answer this question.

_____

_____

4. Do you have any language that could be misinterpreted as an offensive stereotype? Again, check your essay to answer this question.

_____

_____

5. Check your use of masculine pronouns meaning "he" to make sure you are including both men and women. Are there other spots where one gender could feel slighted?

_____

_____

6. Are all references to race, religion, sexual orientation, and gender roles necessary in your essay? If not, replace them with references that relate more to your topic.

_____

_____

7. Are you up-to-date on the most widely accepted terms to refer to groups? Check yourself on this, because it isn't something you will know unless you ask at least three others who are well read on current events.

_____

_____

Section IV

Revising

I do an enormous amount of revising. I think of that quote from Valery,
"A poem is never finished, only abandoned." —W.H. Auden

I grew up with the exact wrong idea about writing. I believed that if I were a good writer, I wouldn't have to work at it, that writing was a divinely bestowed gift doled out in a lottery-style fashion. Some would receive it, some wouldn't. Good writers, I thought, let the words roll off the pen with ease and tranquility. In other words, revision equaled failure.

Where did I get such a dumb idea? To be honest, it was all around me. Teachers complimented the "talented" ones in class, confirming the notion that one either had "it" or didn't. My friends with high grades would brag about how they wrote the essay while eating their breakfast just that morning. Also, in high school, there wasn't time for much revision. Usually, I had three hours of homework every night after seven hours of school. An assigned essay would have to be done on Saturday or Sunday. My first draft was often my only draft and rarely did the teacher require multiple drafts.

Even with this major misperception being reinforced at school, the place where I mainly fostered this faulty idea that the talented only write one draft was at home. My brother played sports throughout school, and I spent many Friday nights sitting on cold, metal bleachers. I would not dare leave, not wanting to miss a throw or the fans screaming his name. A few times people grew angry over a missed pass, but what I remember were the compliments. Phrases such as "God given talent," "natural athlete," and "the boy's got something special" all emphasized this idea that one's destiny was predetermined.

Either I would write a good essay if I were naturally good at writing—or I would never.

It wasn't until I was eighteen and showed a new boyfriend a poem that I'd written did I have my epiphany. It was our second date. We'd gone out for coffee, and feeling very adult about drinking caffeine, I did the next adult thing I knew: invited him back to my parent's house. There, I presented him with a poem that I'd written, my method of wooing prospective suitors. Usually, the guys would nod and say something profound such as, "Cool," and then I'd get asked out again. Easy. It was almost as if I were talented in this business of writing poems.

This guy listened quietly as all the others had, keeping his eyes on his shoes. But he was doing something different, nodding his head in appropriate places, making small sounds like, "Hmmm." Once I finished, I looked up at him and prepared my face for all the compliments praising my natural, raw talent that I was about to receive. I knew not to smile too much, of course, because that would appear conceited. I settled for a tilt of the head and poetic stare into the distance.

He said, "You would be pretty good if you would revise."

That comment hit me harder than a punch in the nose on a cold day. Revise? Me?! My first impulse was that I should quit writing, seeing as how I was obviously not any good at it. Maybe I would try painting instead. Then, I got mad and decided to follow his advice. Of course the poem was better after the second draft, and I started to revise more and more until it became part of my process.

But the real question is what did I do with that boyfriend? I married him. That was my second epiphany of the day.

The first epiphany was this: Good writers revise. Bad writers do not. It's as simple as that. But as Patricia O'Conner says, "Revising is more than fixing what's wrong; it's making what's passable better." For example, revising can make a "C" paper an "A" paper.

It is important to note that editing is not revision. Editing is that last polish you do when you are checking for typos and mistakes. Revising is the real work of the essay, but often where people fail to put their time. When you revise, you are ruthless, willing to cut what you love and write in the difficult paragraphs. From the Latin word that means "visit again," revising is exactly that. Visiting your work as if it were your dream house under construction—is the floor plan ideal, do the design elements flow? Rework and rewrite until the essay meets your expectations.

One of the many reasons why I emphasize revising is this is where one learns to write. All through high school, I wrote essay after essay, receiving the same grades and committing the same errors. I thought that just by writing more, I'd get better. Wrong. Piano teachers know this. That's why they stress moving slowly through the scales and learning them correctly, because "practice doesn't make perfect; practice makes permanent." Too often, if you do the same thing wrong over and over, it becomes habit. Think of the times when you have gotten lost going to a friend's house. Often, you take that same incorrect route again until you put a conscious effort into changing.

As you read through this section and find exercises that require a lot of work, remember that this is supposed to be the difficult part of your essay process. And if you need any more convincing that revision is where a writer earns his money (or his grade) remember this: Dickens first named Tiny Tim, Puny Pete.

21
Topic Sentences

Has a stranger ever come up to you and just started talking? Maybe you're in a check-out line, and the woman behind you notices that you're buying a turkey and says, "Is it a tom or a hen? Because you surely don't want a hen."

This exact scenario happened to me. Other than trying to figure out if I had a male or female block of frozen bird before me, I was also trying to figure out who this lady was with the bright orange lipstick talking turkey. Essentially, I couldn't focus on what she was saying because I didn't understand why she was talking to me in the first place or what her point might have been.

Having a paragraph without a good topic sentence is a lot like this crazy lady at the check-out line. Readers get confused if writers just launch right into their attacks. The reader needs a good topic sentence to understand what writers will be talking about in the next paragraph and why. With a good topic sentence, the reader's attention can be on your persuasion abilities rather than trying to decipher what you will be talking about. For example, that crazy lady later told me that a hen tends to be tougher than a tom, and obviously, my mother had never taught me that because it looked to her like I was buying a hen.

If you want to make your professor proud, learn how to write topic sentences. I know that the phrase "topic sentences" is familiar to you, but it may be stored deep in your mind's recesses, something you heard in English class as you daydreamed out the window. Simply, a topic sentence is the first sentence of a paragraph. But more than being the first sentence of a paragraph, the topic sentence has to be the leader of the paragraph. A topic sentence succinctly explains what your paragraph is going to discuss and clarifies to the reader what you will say. Also, topic sentences are important for a not-so-good reason, too. Sometimes people skim your work, whether it be an application or a letter to the editor, and when they skim, they often read topic sentences only. Therefore, they must be clear and explain what your essay is discussing. Try the following exercises to help improve your topic sentences.

Exercise 1: Big Umbrella

For this exercise, underline each paragraph's topic sentence. Then, ask yourself if it completely explains what the paragraph is going to discuss. If it does not, rewrite the topic sentence.

Next, exchange essays with a friend. Have him/her read your paragraphs and tell you what the main point of each paragraph is. Check your topic sentence or recently written sentence to see if it accurately reflects the other reader's perception.

Once you have the paragraph's main idea clearly communicated, edit for the following:

1. Does the topic sentence transition well between paragraphs?
2. Do all sentences in your paragraph work to support the topic sentence? A more metaphorical way to view a topic sentence is to picture a giant umbrella hanging over your paragraph, everything unified and dry below it.
3. The topic sentence should say what the paragraph is about and relate to your thesis statement in some way, ideally to support it. Does your topic sentence achieve both goals?

Exercise 2: Stones in the Beans

Once you have written your topic sentence, you need to look at the sentences in the paragraph and make sure that they all belong there. Sometimes a sentence belongs in another paragraph (or the trash can) and is throwing off your entire organization. So, read your sentences in each paragraph and make sure they all fit with your topic sentence. Just like finding one stone in a bowl of bean soup, one out-of-place sentence can mess up your paragraph.

Exercise 3: Back to the Thesis

As you have heard in many of your classes, the thesis is important. While some students feel burdened by the thesis, the thesis is actually your saving grace. Your thesis tells readers to judge your essay by whatever you have outlined in your thesis and only that. For example, if you are writing about the benefits of landing on Mars, your thesis tells readers that you will be talking about that subject and only that subject. The reader should not expect anything else such as a discussion on what the international community might say about it. The thesis defines your essay and establishes parameters by which your essay will be judged.

Because the thesis is so important, you must make sure the reader is convinced that you are supporting it at all times. For this exercise, revisit your topic sentences and make sure each one directly states how it supports the thesis or develops an aspect of the thesis in some way.

Exercise 4: Clearing Thy Throat

Beware. Almost every student writer at one point began with the words, "In today's society. . . ." I call this the throat clearing sentence. You're not sure what to say. You know it needs to be good. You also want to let your readers know why your topic is important, and so presto, we have, "In today's society."

All I can say is resist this temptation. Sometimes, the second sentences of paragraphs are better than the first sentences. The reason is some writers fill the first sentence with what they think they should say or they are simply trying to figure out what to say. The second sentence, however, is filled with what they want to say. Therefore, that's the better sentence. For example, read the following passage and notice how the first sentence is too vague and unnecessary:

> Concerns about one's health are common. Every day one hears reports about new diets, new breakthroughs, and new reasons for being overweight, but one needs to judge these reports carefully. A few questions one should ask are: how many people participated in the study; how long did researchers test their results; and what other reports support the new findings?

A simple deletion of the first sentence would make the entire paragraph better focused.

For this exercise, check all of your first sentences in every paragraph. See if you are doing some fancy throat clearing in the first sentence and read that second sentence to see if it is actually better. (Be sure, however, that you are not taking away the topic sentence that informs the reader what the paragraph discusses.)

22
Structure and Organization

We've all been there. Despite our best efforts to organize and outline, an essay takes on a life of its own once we sit in front of the computer. When you start to revise your essay, you will find yourself working on structure and organization. This isn't necessarily a sign that you weren't organized enough in your drafting stage, but more of a sign that different problems emerge the more you work on a project. The exercises in this chapter will help you structure your essay after you have already written a draft or two where structural problems occurred that you couldn't previously predict.

With writing, each draft will present new issues and complications, and there may come a point where you feel overwhelmed. It is at this point, when you are at the edge of a mess and the beginning of a finished product, that you will probably feel the most negative about your essay.

But let me say this: these feelings are normal. Now is the time to bring in your critic and give yourself a little push. Remember why you felt the urgency to write about this topic in the first place. Take a look at the following exercises and see which ones would most help you—and then do them!

Exercise 1: Writing Outline in Reverse

To figure out where your organization goes awry, you need to first figure out what you have done. For this exercise, write one sentence that summarizes each paragraph's point. When you finish writing those sentences, analyze them to see if there are any apparent problems and correct them.

Answer in particular the following questions:

1. Are all similar points grouped together?
2. Is your structure consistent meaning do you adhere to one type of structure? For example, do you switch between chronological order and cyclical in a narrative? In a research essay, do you switch between chunking versus alternating structures as mentioned in chapter twelve?

3. Finally, look at the overall balance. Do you have five paragraphs on one point and only one paragraph on an equally important point? Does one minor point take up too much space? The given space in an essay equals its importance; make sure your essay reflects your values.

Exercise 2: Mapping

This exercise is one of the most valuable in the book because it can easily boost your grade. Let me tell you how. For this exercise, begin with the second paragraph and read all of your topic sentences. Once read all together, they should sound like your essay, but in miniature form. For example, the following three sentences are topic sentences from three different paragraphs in *Letter from Birmingham Jail* by Martin Luther King, Jr. Notice how the topic sentences make perfect sense next to the other:

> We decided to set our direct action program around the Easter season, realizing that with the exception of Christmas, this was the largest shopping period of the year. This reveals that we did not move irresponsibly into direct action. You may well ask, "Why direct action? Why sit-ins, marches, etc.? Isn't negotiation a better path?"

Don't those sentences sound like they form their own paragraph? If your topic sentences are written well and your organization is correct, all of your topic sentences will flow together like King's so that upon reading only your essay's topic sentences, they will sound like a summary of your essay. You do, however, probably have to do some editing to make the topic sentences flow.

Read your topic sentences and draw a star next to the ones that do not sound as if they came directly from the previous topic sentence. You can have many different reasons for mismatched topic sentences, so read over the following list to see what might be causing the trouble with the topic sentence.

1. You do not have a topic sentence that accurately summarizes your paragraph. (This is usually the problem.) If this is the problem, write a new topic sentence.
2. Your topic sentence is actually the second sentence of the paragraph. Sometimes writers simply have to warm up to what they want to say. If this is the case, delete the first sentence.
3. Maybe your topic sentence is the last sentence of the previous paragraph. If this is the case, move it.
4. The paragraph is actually out of order. Look to see where it would be better placed.
5. Maybe you simply need a word or two that transitions the previous paragraph into the new one. See if there is a phrase that you could add that would help transition your paragraphs. For example, you could say,

"Other than the economic reasons that I have mentioned in the last paragraph, one should consider the moral implications as well." Also, refer to chapter thirty on transitions if you need more help.

6. You simply might have a rare exception that prohibits the two topic sentences from sounding good next to each other. But when I say rare, I mean as rare as winning the lottery's jackpot, so sparingly use this exception.

Once you have fixed what you need to fix, your essay will read much better and clearer. The goal is for your combined topic sentences to sound like the executive summary of your essay. This distillation of your points helps you know the essay is tightly focused and clear. Also, this helps your essay in an indirect way. Sometimes, when a professor is deciding what grade to give you and reads back over your work, it is typically the thesis statement and topic sentences that will be examined with more scrutiny. If your topic sentences sound complete, fluid, and clearly related, you will earn the higher grade.

Exercise 3: Color Code

If your essay feels like a tornado has ripped through it and scattered all of your thoughts, I suggest you revert to a tried and true technique: coloring. Grab a fistful of a different colored crayons or highlighters and assign each distinct idea in your essay a color. For example, on an essay discussing going to war with a country, any ideas discussing economic issues would be highlighted pink, while any ideas discussing moral issues would be yellow, etc. In the end, the goal will be to move "like colors" together so that everything pink will be in one paragraph and everything highlighted yellow will be in another paragraph and so on. This exercise works well in prewriting also. Once you have completed this fundamental reorganization, complete the mapping exercise.

Exercise 4: Kill Your Darlings

I used to have the same problem with all of my essays. They were disjointed, unorganized, and nothing was explained properly. In other words, I drove a few teachers mad. My problem, however, was actually a good one. I had too many ideas.

Having a lot of ideas can lead to complex, insightful essays. It's a sign that the writer is excited and trying to push the essay into new territory. What has to be done to make the essay succeed is a drastic measure called "kill your darlings." I've heard fiction writers use this term the most often, usually when they have tried and tried to incorporate a certain scene, a certain character—and nothing will work. Perhaps the character doesn't appear vital to the story-line or the scene never transitions well. Simply, the writer must kill his darlings which means the writer must be willing to cut out that which he loves if it hurts the overall piece.

I see many a good essay ruined because the writer is too excited and couldn't stop himself from adding a tenth potential essay topic in his two page essay. Just like thinning young plants from the garden, we have to cut the weaker ideas, even if they're interesting, to make room for the essential points to fully develop.

If despite your best efforts, your essay remains unclear and unsubstantiated, it's time to kill your darlings. Delete a few of your weaker points and then spend more time explaining the points that are left.

Exercise 5: Long-Winded

Do your paragraphs tend to run long? After your first draft, read over the essay looking for large blocks of black ink. If you see a black blot on the page, ask yourself if you can divide up that massive block into something more manageable, something called paragraphs. Make sure, though, to create a new topic sentence if necessary when you divide up your paragraphs.

Also, do you have some skinny paragraphs? Overall, your paragraphs need some sort of uniformity in length, so add to the short paragraphs and divide up the long ones.

Exercise 6: Revisit Aristotle

The great rhetorician Aristotle believed that one needed a balance of logic and emotion to persuade the reader. Facts that persuade relate to logic and anecdotes relate to emotion. (Simply giving one's opinion is not considered a fact.)

Outside of every paragraph write the elements that are present: logic or emotion. You should have more of logic than emotion. If emotion dominates your essay, you know your essay is relying on personal anecdotes and emotions too much. Aristotle believed (and so do I) that an essay needs to have both elements to persuade, but one ultimately persuades with logic and facts rather than emotional techniques.

Chapter 23
Voice

All too often what is missing in voice is confidence.

—*Julia Cameron from* The Artist's Way

Sometimes I write on a student essay, "Strong voice." I wonder, though, if the student knows what I mean since voice is such an elusive quality. In writing, the quality that makes your writing sound different from anyone else's writing is called your voice. Being able to tap into your voice, your true authentic voice, separates writers into the great category versus the good category. In other words, would you rather sound like everyone else and be an imitator, or would you rather connect with your true voice and be an innovator? Discovering your true voice is something like having a conversation with a friend or stranger who brings out your best, someone who encourages you to be authentic and thoughtful. You can recognize that feeling just as you can recognize when you are "putting on airs" which is the opposite of using your true voice. For essay writing, you want to capture that feeling you have when you walk away from a conversation feeling as if you presented yourself in an honest, unique, and authentic way.

To discover your own voice, you have to uncover your authenticity. Usually, when a student is not taking advantage of his true voice, he is trying to sound like someone else. Perhaps the student wants to sound like an adult, the professor, or the kid in class who is making the "A" (and who subsequently has already discovered his voice). Voice is a combination of diction, syntax, and persona. It is your personality revealed through your choice of words and the arrangement of those words. Sound simple enough? Well, it's not. It takes confidence. It requires paying attention to other writers' voices. It also demands practice. Try a couple of the following exercises to help you discover your voice.

Exercise 1: Dear John

We all have heard of those "Dear John" letters where the wife leaves her husband and informs him of this through a letter propped up on the family mantel. While some could claim leaving a letter is a harsh and cowardly way to leave a spouse, some people cannot explain their true feelings if they feel a bit threatened. Writing letters allows those people a way to find their authentic voice and say what they feel. While I do not recommend leaving a spouse, much less via a letter, I do recommend trying to communicate your thoughts in a clear manner that is honest and authentic.

For this exercise, I want you to look at an essay that you are working on and find a place where you didn't completely express your thoughts. Take one particular point and rewrite it now, practicing how your voice sounds on the page without fear of reprisal. Write as you feel compelled to write, but avoid profanity. Once you have finished, take a look at what you wrote and compare it to the earlier version. Which voice sounds more like you? Which voice sounds better?

Exercise 2: A Word on Originality

The root of the word originality is origin, meaning something that has come from you. Marvin Bell, a well known poet, said that "originality is a new amalgam of influences" meaning that originality is the unique mix of one's personal experiences and ideas. The point of this exercise is to help you see that voice is in a large part perception and accurately portraying that perception. For this exercise, think of an event that happened in your childhood that both you and a sibling would remember. (If you don't have a sibling, think of a close childhood friend.) Write your memory of that event. Then, write in your sibling or friend's voice his/her memory of that event. What details would the other person choose? What details would you choose? How will the description of the event be different? How will the rhythm of the speech be different?

When you are finished, the goal is to have captured two distinct voices on the page.

24
Citations and Quotations

College students will not graduate without having spent many hours researching and integrating quotes into their required essays. Other than the secret belief that professors love to assign research essays to inflict pain and stress upon their students, professors have good reasons why students must research and provide quotes. Ideas are built upon previous ideas, just like a brick in a house is laid upon another brick until finally one builds a mansion. Einstein, heralded as one of our most brilliant minds, often developed his "new" theories by combining or altering previous ideas. For example, Einstein based the famous $E=MC^2$ principle off of two balance principles that already held a high place in pre-relativity physics. Without research, Einstein would never have discovered a new level of physics just as your essays would never be as deep or complex without research.

We research to educate ourselves, to support our opinions, and to build upon the ideas before us with the hope of developing something new. Of course we have to cite our information and quotes and plainly state where we get our information because ideas have value in our society. I love the fact that in a culture that many complain is materialistic and money-grubbing, we still believe that intangibles such as art, music, literature, and ideas are valuable and belong to the creator.

While I will not explain the rules for MLA and APA seeing as how there are many excellent grammar books that cover that topic, I do have a few points to make that will help reinforce the quotes you add to your essay

Exercise 1: Raisins in a Bagel

Just how often should one use direct quotes in an essay? Honestly, the answer to that question will vary depending on the subject and the professor, but almost all professors despise those essays that are simply quote after quote after quote. Essays burdened with too many quotes give readers the impression that the writer did not have any thoughts on his own. Frankly, it is sometimes difficult to tell if the student even understood what he was quoting.

One wants to have a good balance of quotes and original ideas. But this requires a shift in thinking; you are no longer that dumb student who doesn't know anything. In college, the people you quote are there to support what you say, what you believe, what you propose. In other words, you are in charge of your essay, not the leading scientist that you might be quoting on mad cow disease. Yes, the scientist probably knows more about mad cow disease than you do, but this is your essay, and the reader is paying attention to your thoughts.

To find the right balance, think of eating a raisin bagel with the quotes being the raisins. You won't get a raisin in every bite, but the raisins are there to accent the bagel. Quotes work this way, too.

Take a look at your essay and see if you are in charge or if your quotes are in charge. If you find that you have too many direct quotes, see if you can paraphrase that information or add in more of your thoughts.

Exercise 2: Proper Introductions

Have you ever invited a friend over only to have him show up with a girl whom he doesn't introduce? They smile and say hello. You say hello back. Your friend talks about this cool band he heard last night while he grubs through your fridge and finds a drink for the girl. They plop down on your sofa and ask what's good on television.

The entire time your mind is halfway listening to your friend and halfway thinking, "Who is she?" Your friend needed to properly introduce her immediately, saying, "This is Tina, my cousin, and my mom asked me to show her around town." Otherwise, you're not quite paying attention to what's happening, but just wondering who is this person drinking your root beer.

In an essay, one needs to have proper manners, just like your mother always told you. When you give a direct quote in an essay, you need to tell the reader who is the person speaking. Is it Uncle Billy from his Web site or a well-regarded expert on the subject? By using proper introductions, your reader can simply concentrate on the point of the quote without wondering who is speaking or what is the person's credentials.

Whenever you give a direct quote, you are doing more than plugging in a quote, but in fact, you have three responsibilities for every one direct quote. You must introduce the person speaking, provide the direct quote, and then translate the quote. Translating the quote is also the "so what" or "what this quote means to me" sentence. By translate, I mean that you must tell me the point to take from the quote that you provided. Never assume the reader will simply get the brilliant point that supports your brilliant thesis.

For this exercise, find a direct quote where you need to add either a proper introduction and/or a translation sentence after the quote.

Student Sample:
(Notice how this writer provides the three necessary steps when using a direct quote: introduction, quotation, and translation.)

Some advice from a manager of a well known reggae group, Toots and Maytails, changed my life. I told him I was determined to be famous one day. He said to me, "Don't crave the fame. Crave the inspiration. Because if you aim to inspire, the fame will come." I realized that devoting all my efforts to being in the glamourous limelight was extremely self-centered and neglectful of other career opportunities.

—Katherine Shelley

Exercise 3: The Buddy System

Where MLA or APA documentation is concerned, no one can claim artistic license. In other words, how you format the reference or works cited page should look exactly like every other college student's across the country. For all the different philosophies and pedagogies students will encounter at college, citing one's sources and writing the reference page is probably the one aspect of education where everyone agrees. Yet, there are many opportunities for mistakes. Is your period in the right spot? What about those quotation marks? And just how do you cite a Web site? Well, there are clear, concrete answers to all of this.

To make sure that my students are using correct MLA, I have them compare their in-text citations and works cited page with a classmate's or with a sample. Everyone's essay should look exactly the same when it comes time for citations. For this exercise, switch essays with someone and make sure that the citations look exactly like your citations.

25
Abstract versus Specific Writing

A paradox exists in writing. Writers love to think in abstract terms, yet readers crave concrete detail. An abstract term is anything that one cannot hold or touch such as fear, love, or greatness. We especially use abstract terms when we are talking about broad topics such as religion, justice, and society. Readers, however, prefer the specific, visible representations of abstractions such as words like heart (for love), king (for greatness), and ghosts (for fear). I could tell you why this is in abstract language, but the following exercise will show you why—in specific terms—readers love specifics and why abstract concepts made concrete are less likely to confuse readers.

Exercise 1: What Do You See?

Step One

You will see a list of words below and for each word, write down the first word, and I mean the very first word, that comes to your mind no matter how silly. For example, if I say frustration, you may think of your roommate or, for whatever reason, broccoli. Quickly write down whatever association the following words trigger and then quickly move on to the next word until you have finished with the list.

Love: _____

Justice: _____

Hate: _____

Cowardice: _____

Wealth: _____

Stupidity: _____

Bravery: _____

Step Two

Look over your answers. Each of the words in the previous list was an abstract term. Notice how often you provided a specific example after each of those abstract words. For instance, did you write heart or name a person for the abstract term "love"? For "cowardice," did you write lion or name a person? Most people will reply with almost all specific examples. (If you did not, understand that you think in abstract terms and will have to work a little harder than others to provide specific examples.)

One reason why readers crave specifics rather than abstracts is that the mind often functions with visuals. As the previous list revealed, usually when someone gives an abstract term, like love, a picture will flash in the mind. I picture my husband. I don't plan on doing this. It is simply how the mind processes information. Perhaps the reason for this is we learn a lot of language through visuals. Before you could speak well as a toddler, when your mother held out a glass of juice to you and said, "You want juice?" your mind associated the visual of a slender glass of orange stuff with the sound "juice," and language was born for you.

As adults, we do not change much. We still need something to see after an abstract word, something to "sink our teeth into." Otherwise, readers may not quite understand what it is you are saying, especially considering how different people's perceptions can be. That's why when you leave an idea in the abstract, someone will ask, what do you mean?

My solution to avoid being overly abstract is to back up every abstract idea with a specific example. Providing a specific example after your abstract idea or term helps readers to know exactly what you mean. You could provide abstract concept after abstract concept in your essay, and the reader will simply fill in the blanks himself, but this is your piece of writing. Control what the reader sees.

Read the following example from E.B. White's "Once More to the Lake" and notice how he begins with an abstract phrase and then provides specifics to direct the reader's imagination:

> Summertime, oh, summertime, pattern of life indelible, the fade-proof lake, the woods unshatterable, the pasture with the sweetfern and the juniper forever and ever, summer without end; this was the background, and the life along the shore was the design, the cottages with their innocent and tranquil design, their tiny docks with the flagpole and the American flag floating against the white clouds in the blue sky, the little paths over the roots of the trees leading from camp to camp and the paths leading back to the outhouses. . . .

Exercise 2: For Example

Go through your essay and find abstract words and ideas, underlining them whenever you find them. Then, check to see if you follow the abstract terms with specific examples in the next sentence. If you do not, do so now.

Student Sample:
Abstract statement: Being intuitive to what could be the "new sound" is a thread that sews the artist's style with the producer's technological skill. (Abstract concepts: Intuition and new sound.)
Fact added later: For example, Butch Vig produced Nirvana's "Never-mind," which changed the music style of the 90s. (Specific terms: Butch Vig provides an example of a producer who is intuitive, and Nirvana represents a new sound.)

—Clinton Wilson

Exercise 3: Two Pens

This easy exercise helps you determine if you have enough facts for your essay. With one pen, underline every fact you have provided for your argument. As you do this, you'll have questions about which statements are facts. Numbers are facts. Historical examples are facts. Quotes are facts. Facts are not excerpts from a Web site trying to sell you something or your logical opinions.

Once you have finished underlining your facts, take another color pen and underline the opposition's facts.

At the end of all of this pen marking, you should see some lines in every paragraph except for maybe the introduction and conclusion. If this is not the case, make a note to add more facts to the paragraph that is lacking facts or check to see if this paragraph is an exception to the rule.

Also, look at the colors. Do you see a lot more of one color than the other? You should see more of the color that represents your facts, but the opposition needs facts, too, at least about twenty percent of the total factual examples in your essay. So, take a look at what you have underlined and identify where you need to add more specific examples.

26
Advanced Development

I have always felt that the first duty of a writer was to ascend—to make flights, carrying others along if he could manage it. —E.B. White

In chapter fifteen, which was the earlier chapter on development, we discussed the importance of having your essay showcase your complex, critical thinking. In other words, your essay needs certain elements such as unique ideas to indicate to your professor that you are truly engaged in your topic and that you have offered insight into the issues that we think about daily. This chapter offers suggestions on how you can distinguish your essay from other essays, but the exercises do require at least a first or second draft. Look through all of the exercises and then try one or two exercises that appeal to you.

Exercise 1: Universal Element

In the conclusion chapter, I talked about the importance of having a universal element in your writing. Simply, a universal element means that you have an essay that many people, other than your mother, could care about and love. Gertrude Stein, a well-known poet, explains that she writes for herself and for strangers. In other words, the pleasure of writing is all hers, but she wants people who do not know her to care about what she's saying.

For this exercise, freewrite on why a stranger should care about your essay topic. Once you are done, see what you can apply to your essay from your freewrite. By writing on why a stranger should care, you are bringing the universal element to your essay.

Student Sample:
   (Notice how she moves the essay beyond her personal concern of feeling too young and addresses how many people feel dissatisfied with their age, no matter what it is.)

One thing that I have learned is that I am not alone when I feel like age constantly attacks me. It is almost as if it is a curse that lingers within you and waits for those moments when age is the one issue you are trying to avoid; it is during those moments that it strikes. It has no mercy. When I truly sit and think about it, I can see how age is always an issue and not just for me, for others, too. Whether the issue lies in the fact that you are too young or too old, it seems that people are rarely satisfied with their age. You hear children and teenagers like myself constantly wishing that they were older, and then you have adults who are always in search of the "fountain of youth." There are some things that people just will never be satisfied with, and age is one of them.

—Alayna Sims

Exercise 2: Peeling the Onion

I'm one of the few people who does not mind chopping up an onion. (I wear contacts, the secret weapon against onion tears.) In fact, aside from the culinary aspects, there's something I love about an onion. I like the feel of its papery husk. I like the clean crisp sound it makes when my knife slices it. I like how each ring contains another ring. I like the layers.

I've come to use the term "layers" in my own courses. "You must have layers in your essay," I'll say to my students. What I mean is that they must have their essay's topic connect to other larger issues in order to add good development. For example, one of my favorite essays, "The Clan of One-Breasted Women" by Terry Tempest Williams, first talks about her family's struggle with breast cancer. She then moves the essay beyond herself and her family and speculates that the cause of her family's breast cancer is the nuclear testing that the U.S. government conducted in her home state of Nevada. She then begins talking about the power of government and poses tough questions such as should the government purposely harm a few unknowing citizens in order to secure safety for a majority of the country? With each broader implication, she is adding depth, or my expression "layers," to her essay. This essay moves from the self, to family, to environmental issues, to government, and finally to issues of power and sovereignty.

For this exercise, create two or more layers that could apply to your essay. To do this, ask yourself, what are the larger connections to my topic? If you have absolutely no idea, ask other people to help you brainstorm. Once you have a few questions that could generate some broader implication to your essay topic, try to answer them. Then, add these questions and answers to your essay, either sprinkled throughout it or placed in the concluding paragraph.

Exercise 3: What Did You Learn?

Do a freewrite on what you learned while writing this essay. It could be a fact, an opposing viewpoint, or a perspective you had not heard of before. Maybe your opinion changed on one of the issues you mentioned in your essay. Whatever it was, tell the readers what you learned and explain your learning process in detail for about one paragraph.

Exercise 4: Scaredy Cat

Do a freewrite on some points that you were too scared to bring up in your essay. Don't worry about the reason for now. Write them down and then read what you wrote to see if anything could be added to your essay. Maybe an idea that you thought was too weird or risky could actually help develop your essay.

Student Sample: (In this essay on possible careers, the student felt like his idea was simply too unconventional to mention, but it served as an interesting paragraph that showed the student was truly thinking for himself.)

Given my background so far, it would surprise everyone, including myself, that I am seriously researching becoming a trucker. I like the freedom and adventure, as well as the isolation involved with being a cross-country truck driver. I drive long distances all the time (more weekends than not I'm driving at least sixteen hours) and enjoy all the time I have to think and listen to music. Music never sounds as good as it does in my car. I love the open highways and late night driving; and I already know a lot about different travel routes. My research shows that entry level jobs can start as high as thirty thousand a year, and with experience salaries can grow to upwards of fifty thousand a year. . . .

—Chris Beard

Exercise 5: So What?

I know students think it, and so do professors. The "it" is why does your essay matter? Students might be rubbing their eyes from lack of sleep, yet typing away on an essay due the next day, pushing aside the thought that the essay truly does not matter. For this exercise, instead of telling yourself that essays are to college as shots are to doctor visits, address the issue. It is your duty as a writer to uncover why your essay matters. So, ask the question, "So what?" And for the first time, answer this important question in your essay.

Section V

Editing

As the semester comes to a close, resulting in either cold, bitter days or hot, eager afternoons, I notice a change in my students that is consistent despite the weather changes. The best writers in class come to me surprised, baffled even, that the essays they love and receive good grades for, are taking a long time to write. They say that the more they learn about writing, it seems like the more time they need to write. I smile and tell them the truth: writing is not one of those subjects where the more you know, the faster you can complete the task.

Granted, one can learn shortcuts and learn what types of writing should be done quickly and what types of writing require days and days, but good writers are good not because they spend less time writing than everyone else. They spend more. One starts to realize the many elements to a good essay, and one wants to do them well.

When you get to the editing stage of your essay, understand that this is the final stage and one that usually separates the amateur writing from the professional. In this section, you will find exercises that elevate your writing to one higher level than before. Here, you will edit your essay's rhythm as well as check for typos and spelling errors. You will also work on transitions that can make such a tremendous difference to any essay.

I would like to remind you that you should only use these exercises once you have the draft you are ready to turn in to the professor. The reason is that you don't want to waste time changing the rhythm of a sentence that you may not even include later. Instead, come to this chapter when you feel as if you are finished, and then simply do one more strong edit. Read through the exercises and do as many of them as you can or at least the ones that your essay needs the most.

27
Sentence Structure

I am going to tell you a secret. On the first day of class, when everyone sits up straight in their chairs and nods eagerly at the end of my sentences, there are a couple of students, hands held in their laps, who have registered with a hope that this will be the English class that finally teaches them how to write. These students feel that they can write, but whenever they put their words down, it is never quite good enough, never what they hoped to say. In fact, it sounds simple. To be more specific, their writing makes them sound simple-minded.

Sometimes a student's writing does sound simple, and often poor development is the cause; but there may be another reason and that reason is called poor sentence structure.

To address this issue, you need to first understand what I mean by sentence structure. I'm assuming that you have a vague understanding of what the term is, but that you have a much more vivid recollection of your elementary school lunch box than you do of Miss Grimball's worksheets on sentence structure.

Let's review. The English language has four basic sentence structure patterns, but sometimes students get stuck using the same one time and time again. This structural rut causes dull or overly simple writing because the rhythm is dull.

"An essay has rhythm?" you might be thinking. The good ones do. Songs change their rhythm, especially for the chorus, because that rhythmic change seizes our attention. We need rhythmic variety or we tune out the music—or the essay. To create rhythm in an essay, we need a variety of sentence structures so that our essays avoid that simplistic, monotonous tone that *Dick and Jane* books are notorious for using. Look at the following review on sentence structure and do your best to learn the information. Granted, this is not exciting material, but consider it to be your brain vitamin for the day. (Did you know that the brain is the only organ that does not wear out over time, but can actually improve if one pushes it to by, hypothetically speaking, memorizing boring sentence structure patterns?)

The Four Basic Sentence Structure Patterns

1. Simple Sentence: The tried and not so true sentence. The structure is a combination of the subject + predicate. (A subject is what the sentence is about and consists of one or more nouns or pronouns. A predicate will be a verb that asserts or asks something regarding the subject.) A subject and predicate allows the sentence to stand alone. This pattern is also called an independent clause.

> **Example:** Sally likes English class essays.

2. Compound Sentence: This sentence contains two or more independent clauses and does not have a dependent clause. You may join the two clauses with a semi-colon or a comma paired with a coordinating conjunction. (A coordinating conjunction is: and, or, nor, but, yet, for, so. FANBOYS is a good a mnemonic device.)

> **Example:** Sally likes English class essays, and Sally likes drinking glue.

3. Complex Sentence: This sentence contains one independent clause with at least one dependent clause.

> **Example:** Sally likes English class essays because Sally likes drinking glue.

Or, you can also write that as a dependent clause + a comma + independent clause.

> **Example:** Because Sally likes drinking glue, Sally likes English class essays.

4. Compound-Complex Sentence: This sentence consists of two or more independent clauses and at least one dependent clause. There are many different groupings and possibilities for this sentence type.

> **Example:** Seeing as how Sally likes drinking glue, we might not want to trust Sally's opinion concerning English class essays, and we definitely don't want to trust her opinions concerning where to stop for a refreshing drink.

Exercise 1: Simple Sam

Let's practice varying sentence structure using a paragraph from a student who uses and abuses the simple sentence (subject + predicate) construction time and time again. This is the first type of sentence construction that you are taught as a child, and sometimes when a student feels like he has to have perfect grammar, he'll revert to this type so as not to make mistakes. But that "solution" causes other problems.

Student Example in Need of a Makeover:
Frederick Schilling is an Arab historian who believes that Palestine should be an Arab state. He bases his opinion on the fact that Arabs are indigenous to the area. He believes that because the Arab's connection with Palestine dates back to the very earliest of times, the land should be given over to them.

Did you really read that passage or skim it? True, the passage is dull, but that is largely because of the sentence structure. (Notice how every sentence starts off with a subject, either the word "Frederick" or "He".) Now, I will rewrite that passage changing only the sentence structure, and I want you to notice how much better it sounds.

Rewrite:
Basing his opinion on the fact that Arabs are indigenous to the area, Frederick Schilling, an Arab historian, believes Palestine should be an Arab state. Since Arabs' connection with Palestine dates back to the very earliest of times, the land should be given over to them.

The difference is substantial, yet I changed only the sentence structure. When you want to vary the structure in your own writing, you will first have to allow for a moment of mess and potential grammar mistakes until you find the right construction. Often, writers can flip the sentences, writing the last part first. Or, writers use a transitional phrase such as *in contrast* or *nevertheless*, etc. Third, try dependent clauses: *Because she worked early in the morning*, she had to go to bed early. Finally, use gerunds such as "walking," "riding," or "driving." Now, play around with the following student passage and make it better.

Student Example:
The public hungers for facts from its politicians. This hunger is first determined out of curiosity, but also out of fear that politicians are hiding facts. The scandal of Watergate illustrates how secrets can hurt both society and its leaders.

Rewrite of Student Example:

_____

_____

_____

_____

_____

Exercise 2: A Lesson from Steinbeck

Steinbeck's passages often have a lovely, varied sentence structure. Take a look at the following paragraph from his novel *Cannery Row*:

How can the poem and the stink and the grating noise—the quality of light, the tone, the habit and the dream—be set down alive? When you collect marine animals there are certain flat worms so delicate that they are almost impossible to capture whole, for they break and tatter under the touch. You must let them ooze and crawl of their own will onto a knife blade and then lift them gently into your bottle of sea water. And perhaps that might be the way to write this book—to open the page and to let the stories crawl in by themselves.

What power that paragraph has! Yes, what he is saying is interesting, but it is also his sentence structure that makes this writing so engaging. A typical student, using the same words and same ideas, but a less varied and simpler sentence structure would write that paragraph as so:

The poem is difficult to set down alive. The writer has to describe the stink of the place and the grating noise just right. The writer may want to include the quality of light, the tone, the people's habits and their dreams. Some marine animals such as flat worms are so delicate that they are almost impossible to capture whole. They break and tatter under touch. You must let them ooze and crawl of their own will onto a knife blade. Then, you can lift them gently into your bottle of sea water. I plan to write the book this way. I plan to open the page and to let the stories crawl in by themselves.

Reading those two passages back to back, the difference is jarring. If you look closely, you'll see that I changed very little. In fact, some of the sentences are exactly the same as Steinbeck's sentences. What I did change was his varied sentence structure to a repetitive use of the simple sentence. There is nothing wrong with a simple sentence, and in fact, Steinbeck uses them, but you cannot overuse this sentence or it will dull your writing

Now, take a look at your essay that you are ready to turn in. Go to the middle of the essay and pick one paragraph at random. Identify what type of sentence structure you are using for each sentence. You may find that you already vary your sentence structure which is great, but you will probably also find a clump of subject + predicate sentences. (A clump would be three or more together.) Wherever you see this clump, vary your sentence structure. You don't need to change all of the sentences in the clump, but one or two sentence changes will give your essay the rhythm it needs.

Exercise 3: Parallel Bars

"Give me liberty or give me death."

My guess is you heard that phrase before the age of five and could repeat it yourself before the age of ten. Why is that? The sentiment is good, but would you have remembered it so easily if the phrase were "life is not worth living if one does not have liberty." I'm even bored typing that sentence. The reason why "give me liberty or give me death" is so effective is largely because it uses what is called parallel language, meaning that the series are written in the same grammatical pattern. For example, "Give me liberty or give me death" is parallel because the two series have the same pattern of verb + pronoun + noun. One could also write in parallel language, "Give me liberty or give me applesauce," which is technically correct and memorable because of its construction, but nonsensical.

Use this technique especially when you are presenting many items in a sentence. For example, a student might write, "College students choose their classes based on who is teaching the class, the class time, and what they are interested in or need to study." When you make the language parallel, you would write that sentence like this: "College students choose their classes based on the professor, the class time, and the subject." Not only can parallel language add rhythm, but make phrases more concise, too.

For this exercise, correct the following sentences so that they have parallel language. Feel free to change whatever you need, but make sure that you include all the necessary words such as the prepositions, articles, and the word "to" if you are using an infinitive. My answers are at the end of this chapter, but keep in mind that there are many correct ways to rewrite these sentences.

1. At the slumber party, the girls ate pizza, spent a lot of time gossiping about boys, and eagerly waited for their favorite activity—pillow fights!

    _____

    _____

2. People play sports for many reasons such as recreation, the physical benefits, and the feeling that they are part of a team.

    _____

    _____

3. When I decided to buy an SUV, I knew it was not fuel efficient, but I bought it because of its look, because it performs well in the snow and rain better than a car, and for its all-wheel drive.

    _____

    _____

4. The cheerleader jumped, yelled, and was tumbling throughout the game.

_____

_____

5. When working on an essay, have a friend in school read it or someone who is good at essays.

_____

_____

6. The wise man aspires for great achievements and also should plan for unexpected set backs.

_____

_____

*Now that you have practiced on these sentences, find 2-3 sentences in your essay that could use parallel language

Exercise 4: Fancy Pants

One type of sentence called the periodic sentence leaves an impact when used well. The periodic sentence, or "fancy pants" sentence as it is known in elite circles, gets its power by purposely placing the subject and predicate at the very end of the sentence. Take a look at the following example by the poet John Milton from *Paradise Lost* to see how the sentence is constructed:

> Of Man's first Disobedience, and the Fruit
> Of that Forbidden Tree, whose mortal taste
> Brought Death into the World, and all our woe,
> With loss of Eden, till one greater Man
> Restore us, and regain the blissful Seat,
> Sing, Heavenly Muse, that on the secret top
> Of Oreb, or of Sinai, didst inspire
> That Shepherd, who first taught the chosen Seed,
> In the Beginning how the Heavens and Earth
> Rose out of Chaos.

For this exercise, write a periodic sentence as your concluding sentence. That way, the periodic sentence will not confuse readers who should be well familiarized with your topic by now. I suggest that you take the conclusion sentence that you already have and simply edit it.

ANSWERS TO EXERCISE 3: PARALLEL BARS

1. At the slumber party, the girls ate pizza, gossiped about boys, and planned for their pillow fight.
2. People participate in sports for many reasons such as for recreation, health, and comradery.
3. When I decided to buy an SUV, I knew it was not fuel efficient, but I bought it for its style, performance, and all-wheel drive.
4. The cheerleader jumped, yelled and tumbled throughout the game.
5. When working on an essay, have a friend who is in school or someone who is good at essays read your work.
6. The wise man aspires for great achievements and plans for unexpected set backs.

28
Sentence Length

The sentence is the most basic tool offered to a writer, yet we rarely think about its length. All writers, however, can improve their writing by making conscious decisions of when to use long sentences versus short sentences. A good mix of sentence lengths improves your essay's rhythm and adds energy to your writing.

Short sentences have a personality all their own. They can be punchy. Direct. Decisive. Or, they can imply that the writer is going for a tired, tedious vibe, which may or may not be intended. They can, if used incorrectly, leave a drab feeling if they are put in too often and too close together.

A long sentence can build on its own energy, just like a wave developing far off shore, growing bigger and bigger until it finally crests—and then crashes. Novelist William Faulkner is known for writing sentences that run long, but sometimes the reader can get lost mid-sentence if not handled with care.

In the end, the writer needs to be in control of his craft, creating effects by choice, not chance.

Exercise 1: Uncovering Your Habits

To first improve your skills, you need to know how long you typically write your sentences. Go to a paragraph in the middle of your essay and count the number of words per sentence. Keep a tally of the number of words per sentence, and then fill out the chart below.

How many sentences had 1-5 words?   _____

How many sentences had 6-11 words?   _____

How many sentences had 12-17 words?   _____

How many sentences had 18-24 words?   _____

How many sentences had 25-30 words?   _____

How many sentences had 31 words or more?   _____

Now it is time to analyze your results. I've found that most student writers hover in the 12-24 range. Try to vary from that expected length and incorporate very long and very short sentences so that you can have a good variety. (Consider joining some sentences for longer ones and dividing up others.) You may need to look at two or three paragraphs to get an accurate view of your habits. Once you have finished figuring out your normal patterns, make the necessary changes to your work.

Exercise 2: Sunday Morning Sermons

Preachers can be great orators as was the Reverend Martin Luther King, Jr. With parishioners sometimes too warm, too crowded, and too hungry, preachers have learned how to hold our attention. One technique they use is having a long sentence go and go and go until finally it ends; then, a short sentence follows it. Take a look at the example from King's *Letter from Birmingham Jail*. Notice how he builds the tension and then purposely lets it fall hard for a memorable effect:

> In spite of shattered dreams of the past, I came to Birmingham with the hope that the white religious leadership of the community would see the justice of our cause and, with deep moral concern, serve as the channel through which our just grievances could get to the power structure. I had hoped that each of you would understand. But again I have been disappointed.

Create a tension like King's in your own essay. Write a long sentence of over thirty words followed by a short sentence of under six words at the end of a persuasive paragraph.

29
Metaphors and Similes

We all know about metaphors and similes from our study of poetry in high school. We know that similes make comparisons between two objects with a "like" or "as" (she's as pretty as a rose), and we know that a metaphor also makes a comparison but without "like" or "as" words ("all the world's a stage. . .").

Metaphors and similes are fun, but often students feel as if they cannot insert them in their essays believing that these are techniques reserved for classes like creative writing. Actually, in any newspaper, you will find at least one simile or metaphor. History books, psychology courses, even a health pamphlet will contain a simile or metaphor. These techniques aren't just for flowery language; they serve to add interest and to clarify one's meaning. Work to include them.

Exercise 1: Fill in the Blank!

Let's practice at writing metaphors and similes. The idea here is to fill in the blank as quickly as you can. Let your mind take long leaps and have fun.

1. He cast his fishing line as if _____ .

2. She signed the divorce papers like _____ .

3. The ground is like the sky when the _____ is
   like _____ .

4. When the runner fell, the pain was _____ .

5. Stephanie phrased the question as if _____ .

6. Hate is to a dark cave as love is to _____ .

7. There was no end to her love, although it burned _____ .

8. The man fell asleep on the park bench as if _____ .

9. A student in _____ is like a baby in _____ .

10. The _____ of night is a _____ .

Exercise 2: Pick a Profession's Verbs

I use this exercise to make my language striking or "fresh." Again, this exercise will give you practice at metaphors and similes.

Step One
Pick a profession. For example, chef, policeman, meat packer, etc.

_____

Step Two
List ten verbs that would be common of that professional. For example, if you picked chef, write cut, dice, cook, simmer, taste, salt, stir, julienne, etc.

1.

2.

3.

4.

5.

6.

7.

8.

9.

10.

Step Three

List ten nouns that are mentioned in your essay. For example, if you are doing an essay on how high school classes need to start later so that teenagers can get more sleep, list alarm clock, morning, sleep, students, etc.

1.

2.

3.

4.

5.

6.

7.

8.

9.

10.

Step Four

Now, take a verb from the first list and make a sentence with it from the noun list. Granted, these sentences might sound a little odd, but try to use as many similes and metaphors as you can. Do this until you have ten new sentences. Maybe one of these can be included in your essay as a fresh and interesting sentence. (For example: When high school students hear that alarm clock go off, they often want to dice it up and throw it in a frying pan never to be heard from again.)

1. _____

_____

2. _____

_____

3. _____

_____

4. _____

_____

5. _____

_____

6. _____

_____

7. _____

_____

8. _____

_____

9. _____

_____

10. _____

_____

Exercise 3: Just One Bite

Remember how your mother would coax you to eat a food you didn't like by suggesting that you take "just one bite." For this exercise, I want you to add just one simile or metaphor to your essay, no matter the subject. Just try it.

Student Sample:
   A major label music career is like swinging a bat at a piñata. Even if I do hit the technicolor papier-mâché horse, it does not mean that I get all of the sweets; I must share with the fellow party attendees.

—Will Owen

30
Transitions

Recently, I met with a student regarding her essay. This was not our first meeting to work on her essay, but our sixth. Although I usually do not meet with a student so often, she was the type of student who spent hours rewriting, days researching, and weeks agonizing. I figured the least I could do was meet with her once a week.

On this particular meeting, she dropped her essay on my desk and said, "It's awful. I don't know why, but it reads so harsh, so jumbled. I mean, why am I even talking about gun shows for two pages? The essay is on gun control!" I asked why had she talked about gun shows for two of the eight pages of the essay. As she explained that gun shows were representative of the problem with gun control, I took notes.

We worked through her entire essay in that method: I asked why each paragraph was in her essay and she told me. What we then did was put in her answers to my questions as the topic sentences and then wrote transitions to make the essay flow. In one hour, we had changed a mess of an essay into an "A" quality essay—and our only focus had been on topic sentences and transitions.

One cannot divorce topic sentences from transitions because to write an effective transition, we sometimes must rewrite the entire topic sentence. If there is one element, however, that students overlook the most with the essay, I would say it is in the redemptive power of the good transition. A good transition can strengthen your essay, support your thesis, and organize your writing so that the finished product flows seamlessly. Nothing is more disruptive than clunky phrases and big leaps that seem to have come from Mars. Anything that disrupts a fluid reading of your essay seriously detracts from your message, so examine your transitions. They are worth a solid hour of effort.

Exercise 1: Looking Back and Looking Forward

One form of transition is what my classes describe as "Looking Back and Looking Forward." What this phrase means is that the writer reads his paragraph and summarizes it in the concluding sentence, yet he is aware of what he will discuss in the next paragraph. In the end, the concluding sentence of the paragraph summarizes his previous thoughts and sets the stage for the subject shift that will come in the next paragraph. A student sample illustrates this point well.

Student Sample:
    When Lily first came to the honey house the first thing she noticed was that the sisters lived for honey. "Nothing was safe from honey. August said honey was the ambrosia of the gods and the shampoo of the goddesses" (Monk Kidd 84). In the world of honey, the women swallowed a spoonful of honey before bed to put them to sleep and a spoonful in the morning to wake them up. They used it as a disinfectant for cuts, a cure for chapped lips, and even used it in their baths. They took honey to calm their minds, give stamina, and prevent fatal disease. It was constantly surrounding them for every use. Not only was the honey there for practical purposes, it also served as their source of income.
    The main beekeeper, August Boatwright, was the source of income for the ladies in the pink house.

—Samantha O'Keefe

Notice how the last sentence of the paragraph sums up the paragraph, but also prepares for the next paragraph on a main character by using the word "income" in both the concluding sentence and then the following topic sentence. This is quite a skillful transition because the student is having to move from discussing honey to discussing a character, yet she connects the two different subjects with the single word "income."

For this exercise, pick one section of your essay where the paragraphs shift abruptly from one subject to the next. Try the "looking back and looking forward" technique. To do so, ask yourself what the two paragraphs have in common; then, formulate your sentence by reflecting on what the previous topic and the forthcoming topic share. You may have to write two sentences to do this: a concluding sentence and the next paragraph's topic sentence.

Exercise 2: Key Word Transition

This exercise is similar to the previous one, but it does not require as much planning. For this exercise, choose a word that naturally fits into the last sentence of the paragraph, and then use that word again in the first sentence of your next paragraph. Read the following student sample for clarification.

Student Sample: *Notice how the key word here is "Tommy."*
Last line of the paragraph: I never dreamed in a million years that would be the last time I would ever get to see Tommy laughing, smiling, and breathing.
First line of next paragraph: A few hours later, Tommy left his house to take his girl named Debbie home.

—*A.J. Bowley*

For this technique, you need to ask yourself what the two paragraphs have in common and then reduce that commonality to one or two words that you use in both the last line of the paragraph and the first line of the new paragraph. For this exercise, try one key word transition in your essay.

Exercise 3: What's Your Question?

Sometimes, voicing the right question is better than voicing the right answer. What I mean by this is that a question that is precise and probes into an issue can produce insightful passages in your essay. One technique that I love in a student essay is using a question at the end of a paragraph or the beginning of a paragraph to move the essay into new territory. These questions, however, are not the type that your mother asked you as a child such as, "Do you want to clean your room now or would you rather be grounded for the weekend?" The answer to that question is obvious. The answer to questions you pose in your essay should be difficult to answer and should serve as your transition into the new paragraph. For example, in Barbara Kingsolver's essay "Stone Soup" on divorced families, she asks at the beginning of a paragraph: "Why is it surprising that a child would revel in a widened family and the right to feel at home in more than one house?" The answer to this question then provides the subject of her paragraph.

For this exercise, use a question as a transition either at the end of a paragraph or the beginning. Have the question be an honest one capturing either what the opposition might be thinking or what you wish to answer.

Exercise 4: A Little Help from Transitional Words

Writers have relied on many different transitional words to ease the twists and turns their essays may take. Review the following list and then add at least three of these transitional words into your essay where the transition may be a little abrupt.

List of Transitional Words and Phrases

To Indicate a New Example:
For example, for instance, specifically, in fact, to illustrate, indeed, the following example, likewise, similarly.

To Indicate an Opposing Idea:
But, despite, in contrast, on the contrary, still, although, one could say, nonetheless.

To Indicate a Sequence:
Also, again, besides, finally, moreover, next, first, second, third, in addition, now.

To Indicate a Conclusion:
As a result, consequently, so, therefore, accordingly, in conclusion, to summarize, in other words, certainly, finally, indeed.

To Indicate an Admission:
I must concede, I admit, although it may be true, it may appear as though, of course, granted.

31
Word Choice

*The difference between the right word and almost the right word is the
difference between lightning and the lightning bug.* —Mark Twain

Do you want to instantly improve your writing with little to no effort? No,
this isn't a diet infomercial—simply a good piece of advice. Commit now to
never using another cliché (in your writing) for the rest of your life.

What counts as a cliché? Any expression that you have already heard
before. Take this sentence for instance: "We instantly clicked" and when "our
eyes met" I knew that I had found "my soul mate." There's not so much wrong
with using a cliché as there isn't much right with using one. When you use a
cliché, you use somebody else's words that were once so powerful, other people borrowed them because they loved what they expressed. Over the course
of years and use, clichés lose their power and simply become convenient.
What's more, by using a cliché, you lose the opportunity to insert your own
voice. Why do you want to use the same expression that your mother, your
doctor, or your postal worker would use? Is experience exactly the same for
everybody? Of course not. There is a better way to express oneself than to say,
"I'm happy as a clam." And is a sandy clam all that happy anyway?

Exercise 1: The Cliché Police

For this exercise, circle all the clichés in your essay and replace them with
your own thoughts, metaphors and/or similes. Take back the power and
replace somebody else's words with your own voice.

Exercise 2: The Most Overused and Worthless Words

We have approximately 616,500 words in the English language according
to the *Oxford English Dictionary, Second Edition*, making English the language with the most words. With all of those words, I would advocate the dis-
missal of two of them: "very" and "really."

My problem with "very" and "really" isn't personal. I actually like the
words. What I don't like is how writers use them. For example, an aspiring

Hemingway writes, "I was nervous." He rereads that sentence, considers the fact that he hadn't been able to eat all day because he would throw up and realizes "nervous" isn't quite adequate. After all, one gets nervous right before one raises one's hand in class which isn't anything like the nervous this writer was experiencing. So, he adds a very before nervous. The better solution would be to find an entirely new adjective that means "very nervous." With over 600,000 words, that shouldn't be too difficult. How about "panic"; how about "high strung?"

"Really" is another one of those words that we abuse. "I had a really good time," you might tell a friend. Why not say great, wonderful, inspiring, relaxing, or rejuvenating time?

And here is the other reason I dislike seeing these two words. If one uses them at all, one uses them all the time. Trust me. If there is one "very" on a page, there are probably three of them. Just like mice, you don't have only one in your house.

For this exercise, search your essay for these two words: "very" and "really." Take them out and then reword the sentence so that it is really saying what you really, really wanted to say.

Exercise 3: Destroy the Palace

I've done it, too. I've realized that I have used the word "society" four times in an essay and the critic starts to say, "You can't use that word again. It makes you look like you have the vocabulary of a snail." So, out comes the thesaurus and a little bit of creative thinking, and I have inserted "the populace" into my essay. Can you hear the pretension? The idea is to look smarter, but in reality a phrase like "the public" would actually sound better because it doesn't call attention to itself and stick out like a school-bus yellow tie in church. Be careful of that one, meant-to-impress word that sticks out.

Let me also caution you against the other type of "big word affliction." Sometimes a student will take a perfectly good word and try to dress it up. The result is often a more generic and wordy choice. For instance, "snow" is changed to "frozen precipitation."

If the goal of an essay is to communicate, any disruption or distraction needs to be edited out of your writing. Review your essay now and make sure that you are communicating your ideas rather than communicating the fact that you own a five dollar thesaurus.

Exercise 4: Jargon, Fargon

Every group has its own set of words and codes. A sociologist I'm sure can do more with the word "transgender" than I ever could. And a poet could talk forever about iambics and dithyrambs. I understand that occasionally one must speak to one's audience and use a profession's jargon. I caution you, however, not to use these words if you have readers who are not in that field. For example, whenever I receive essays on bands, there are many words specific to a recording session that I do not know. Use them if you must, but be aware that your world is not the same as everybody else's world and explain your key terms. Some people follow the "grandmother" rule which means to explain your terms so that your grandmother could understand them.

For this exercise, take a look at your essay to see if you have any jargon that you need to edit out or explain.

Exercise 5: Take Back Your Authority

Do you want to know what I think? I think that young writers use the words "I think" way too much. In fact, I believe that writers should not use the words "I think" or "I believe." For one, those phrases are wordy because the reader assumes that what you write is your belief unless you indicate otherwise. The real reason why I insist that my students delete those words is that they are qualifiers. They allow young writers to state their opinions and then imply, "But this is just my little ol' opinion, and I would completely understand if you disagree with me."

Ideas are better delivered and received if they have confidence behind them. For example, look at the beginning sentences of this exercise and reread them with the "I think" and "I believe" phrases edited out. Without those words, the opening would sound strong.

After all, if the writer is not fully proud of his ideas, who else will be? So, delete "I think" and "I believe" out of your essay and be proud of your opinions.

Exercise 6: Shifty Soil

This next writing mistake is one that we all make partly because we accept it in casual conversation. We shift, we switch, and we swap tense and person whenever the mood strikes us. For instance, we might type part of the essay in past tense and then change to present. Or we first might speak in first person, then second, then third. Some changes must occur, but overall unnecessary changes sneak their way into formal writing way too often.

Before you turn in your essay, read it over to check for mixed tenses and inconsistent shifts in person.

32
Final Checklist

So I consume laborious hours in fashioning my little song. —Horace

You are almost finished with your essay and what you want more than anything at the moment is to be finished. But let me caution you. Don't throw away all the hours you spent writing this essay to only ruin it by turning in an essay pocked with typos and mistakes. Professors grade harshly against these type of errors, as they should, so take the break you need and then do the following exercises. Think of these exercises as the final sprint at the end of a long run.

Exercise 1: Back to the Basics

This exercise will surprise many writers because it seems like such a no-brainer. Simply, review your assignment sheet. I cannot emphasize how often students do not answer all of the questions on the assignment sheet or fail to do the proper structure. Yes, professors tend to write long assignments, so long in fact you get the idea that they are sitting in front of their computers thinking, "What other questions can I throw in this thing to really impress the students with my intellect and scare them at the same time?" Believe it or not, we actually want you to answer the questions, all of them. Even the big ones. And definitely the small ones. So, take a look at your assignment sheet and read it as if it were the first time you reviewed the assignment. Make sure you have done everything that has been asked of you.

Exercise 2: Check It Off

For this exercise, I want you to create a checklist of what you need to edit before you turn in any essay. First, write down what you often have problems with regarding your essays. For example, if you know you have a problem with wordiness, make a note to check that with every essay. If you don't know what you need to edit, think back to your professor's comments. If you have seen the same comment written three different times, pay attention to that. Once you have this list finished, post it next to your computer. Most importantly, use it!

Example of a Checklist:

1. Reread my topic sentences to make sure they flow.
2. Check the assignment sheet to make sure everything is in my essay.
3. Look for run-on sentences.
4. Take out the words just, very, and really.
5. Have one friend read it.

Exercise 3: Worst Fears at Work

Freewrite on everything you fear is wrong with your essay. Here is the time when you need to allow your critic to have full reign, so write down every negative thought, even the fact that you only have blue ink left in your printer cartridge and you really wanted black ink. Once you have finished your freewrite, resolve the issues you noted. Perhaps you can write about how you can fix those fears or schedule a conference with your professor to discuss them.

Exercise 4: Workshop

A workshop is what forms the backbone to a graduate writing program. No, it's not something filled with sawdust and half finished projects, although the latter part of that statement is correct. A workshop is when you bring in a nearly finished piece of writing and present it to a group of 2-15 people to hear 2-15 different opinions of what could make it better. I use workshops for my writing courses because it familiarizes my students with their peers' work and hones their editing skills. We all know it is much easier to find flaws with someone else than with our self, and the workshop takes full advantage of that fact.

If your instructor doesn't have you do a workshop in class, ask a couple of people to get together and read each other's essays with the goal being to improve everyone's work.

Workshop Rules
1. Be truthful. If it is awful, do not say it is good. But remember that truth without compassion is cruelty. So, say all that you want to say, but in the kindest way possible.
2. Be specific. Don't say, "It needs more facts." Take the writer to the specific sentence where facts are needed.
3. Be supportive. If you can, offer suggestions on how to fix problematic passages because young writers fear uncovering some huge flaw that is simply

unfixable. Let me say, that rarely happens. Usually, one can find a solution to an essay's problem.

4. Read out loud. I suggest that you read the essays out loud to each other. Reading a work out loud instantly reveals wording problems and boring patches to the writer.

Questions to Ask

When you discuss each other's essay, debate what you feel is important, but definitely address the questions I list below.

1. What is the best feature to this essay?
2. What is the worst feature to this essay?
3. What is the writer's main point?
4. Where could the writer support his opinion with more details?
5. What sentences were unclear to you?
6. Review the assignment sheet. Does this essay meet all of the qualifications?

Exercise 5: Read It to Roscoe

This is one of my personal editing checks for every piece of writing. I must read it out loud. When I read my fiction or poetry out loud, I can hear where I get bored, where the writing goes flat. I can instantly find those typos that my mind had been correcting for me. I can also easily hear exactly where I am unclear. Now, you may find it silly to read out loud in an empty room, so what I do is read out loud to a wooden rooster. Roscoe the Rooster is quite the receptive listener. He lets me linger over a paragraph as long as I need. He never even blinks, just stares straight at me as if to say, "Is that the best you can do?"

For this exercise, read your essay out loud, either to yourself, your cat, or your imaginary friend. Whatever you do, listen. Hear when you rush because you are bored or because you don't like what you're saying and fix these passages.

Exercise 6: Mind Your Manners

Just as your mother told you that you must always eat your vegetables, you must always, always, show respect to the opposition. Read through your essay and check your tone. Any time your tone could be perceived as caustic or insulting to the opposition, change it. Beyond tone, look for any times where you made comments such as "How can anyone think like this?" "They are immoral," etc. Remember, it only makes you look bad when you demean or belittle the opposition.

Exercise 7: Reading Backwards

This exercise works best for grammatical and wording errors. What I recommend is that you start reading your essay from the very last sentence and read the essay one sentence at a time back to the beginning. Once you force yourself to read your work without the flow of your language, you will catch those subtle mistakes and typos.

Exercise 8: How Do You Know When You're Finished?

Let me rephrase that question. How do you know when you can stop working because the essay is finished versus when you can stop working because you're tired of the @*&^% thing. Surprisingly, I find that when I'm sick of the @*&^% essay, I'm usually done. Here's a checklist though to help make this decision a little easier in case you are in doubt.

1. You've had two tough critics read it, and they both can't find anything wrong with it.
2. You're fixated on little word changes.
3. You cannot bear to look at it another second AND you've already written four drafts.
4. You feel as if you have accomplished your own goals.
5. You let the essay sit for two days and your changes were minimal.
6. You've completed all the exercises in this chapter.

Section VI

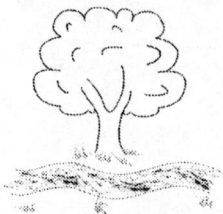

Appendix

33
Favorite Freewrites

If you ever need to blow the dust off your brain and exercise your creative muscles, a freewrite is the perfect elixir. Although I use freewrites throughout the book to help produce good essays, freewrites are also beneficial even when you don't have a project you are working on. Consider them to be the equivalent of a runner's stretch, an exercise designed to keep the muscles flexible and energized, which is why every morning before I write, I begin with a freewrite. So, take a look at this list and write to whatever topic appeals to you at the moment. But remember the freewrite rules: don't stop writing until you reach your page limit; don't shy away from an inappropriate thought; and don't edit yourself.

1. Describe one small activity, like pouring a glass of orange juice, in complete detail.
2. Start off a freewrite with the words, "I remember." When you run out of what to say, do another freewrite beginning with the words, "I don't remember."
3. Describe your first kiss.
4. Write what is around you right now, including sounds and smells as well as visuals.
5. What would you do if you were invisible?
6. Play a song that doesn't have any words and write to the melody. What does the music make you think of? Are you imagining a certain scene, story, or emotion?
7. Think of an emotion, such as happiness, and describe how it feels physically to the body.
8. Write about a place you traveled to a long time ago.
9. Write from the point of view of an object in a kitchen.
10. Pick a line of poetry and begin a freewrite with it.
11. Describe a spiritual experience you have had in detail.
12. What is home to you?
13. What makes you angry?

14. Begin with, "I deny myself . . . ."
15. What is the story surrounding your birth or conception?
16. Describe a time in your life when you felt the most frightened.
17. If you had only one story to tell about your life, what would it be?
18. Think of an activity that you loved doing as a child. Describe it in full detail and how it made you feel.
19. Describe a time in your life when you felt the most alive.
20. Explain how something tastes without using the words "it tastes like. . . ."

34
Guerilla Grammar

You can show a lot with a look. . . . It's punctuation. —Clint Eastwood.

When one writer first told me that she kept a grammar book in the bathroom for quick reading, I thought how strange that was. But then I remembered that when I turned twelve and my hours outside playing turned into hours inside the bathroom primping, my mother posted a list of prepositions to memorize on the bathroom mirror. What is this strange connection with grammar and bathrooms?

I best learn grammar in short little lessons, nothing that takes more than five minutes of concentration. For my classes, I do what I call "Guerilla Grammar" and will give students a quick, unexpected grammar lesson sometime during class. We retain the information best in short bursts of memorization rather than those hour-long lectures in high school. Take a look at the next two exercises and read them on two different days so that you can actually internalize the information presented in them. I also want to add that there are many fine grammar books in libraries and bookstores, and this chapter should not replace further in-depth study for you. Rather, these grammar points are simply the ones I find myself explaining again and again in class.

Exercise 1: Top Ten Grammar Mistakes

1. ITS VERSUS IT'S
This one makes my list for the number one mistake.
"It's" means "It is." Example: It's a rainy day.
"Its" means possession. Example: The bird broke its leg.
Its' does not even exist.

2. HOW ARE YOU? GOOD VERSUS WELL
Most people in the South respond to that question with "I'm good." The grammatically correct answer is saying that you are well. Here is the reason why:
Good is an adjective. Example: The dinner is good.
Well should be used as an adverb. Example: The dinner is going well.

3. THEIR VERSUS THEY'RE AND YOUR VERSUS YOU'RE

The rules for these two are the same as for "its" and "it's."

"Their" and "your" show possession. "They're" and "You're" are contractions. Do not use them unless you mean to say "they are" and "you are."

4. A LOT

"A lot" written as one word does not exist. Only use "a lot."

5. THE SEMI-COLON

Do not use the semi-colon like a comma. It can be used only if what is before and after it is a complete sentence. (See chapter twenty-seven on sentence structure if you need more information on complete sentences.)

The exception to that rule is that the semi-colon may also be used to separate items in a series if the items are each several words long.

6. PRONOUN-ANTECEDENT AGREEMENT

Pronoun-antecedent agreement is not breaking news that will warrant a headline in any newspaper, yet you might see this mistake in a headline. Usually, I find at least one mistake regarding this rule per essay. To have correct pronoun-antecedent agreement, you simply need to make sure that the pronouns and antecedents agree in person, number, or gender. For example, writers will often say something like this: "It is time for every *student* to do *their* part." The sentence needs to read: "It is time for every *student* to do *his* or *her* part." We hate how that his/her sounds, so we write something that is grammatically incorrect such as "their" when we mean only one person. What I recommend to avoid the his/her awkwardness is that you change everything to plural. For example, rewrite that sentence so that it reads, "It is time for *students* to do *their* part."

7. MAY I USE "BUT" TO BEGIN A SENTENCE?

Yes.

But be aware, many will disagree with you. Author of *Words Fail Me*, Patricia O'Conner, explains how this non-rule came into existence. In the eighteenth and nineteenth centuries, this rule (along with a few others such as do not end a sentence with a preposition) began to pop up by classic scholars trying to make our Germanic-based English follow Latin rules. The classic scholars wanted to "civilize the English of Chaucer, Shakespeare, and Milton," is how O'Connor explains it. Essentially, we were trying to turn our language into something it isn't, like dressing up a poodle in a ballerina costume. Some people do it, but that doesn't mean it should become the norm.

So, end your sentences with a preposition, begin them with a but, and have fun driving some English teachers crazy, but understand many will think you are the one who is uneducated.

8. HYPHEN VERSUS DASH

You might be thinking, "Isn't that the same thing?" Nope. First, a hyphen joins two words to create a new meaning such as orange-red or with numbers such as twenty-two. A dash is created on your computer by joining *two* hyphens together. (Some computers create the dash for you if you put the two hyphens together.) The dash's purpose is to serve as a larger pause than a comma. I would like to note that there are no spaces before, between, or after the dash.

Example of a sentence with a hyphen:
The golden-orange sunset instantly calmed me.
Example of a sentence with a dash:
What I am about to say—or what I have been trying to say—is very important.

9. I AM TAKING AN ENGLISH CLASS, A MATH CLASS, A SPANISH CLASS, AND A BIOLOGY CLASS.

The sentence I wrote above is grammatically correct, but when does a student know when to capitalize his class or not? Rules for proper nouns dictate what to do. If you are speaking in general about a course, do not capitalize it. If you are giving the exact course name such as Political Science II, do capitalize it. Languages, and therefore language classes, are always capitalized.

10. WHO AND WHOM

We like how the word "whom" sounds, especially when our English professors use it correctly. The tendency, however, is to use it whenever one wants to sound educated, but one first needs to learn the rules.

In adjective clauses, you look to see what would come after "who" or "whom" to decide what word to use. For example, if a verb follows, you use "who." If the following word is a noun or pronoun, use "whom."

Example:
My grandmother, who is quite wealthy, only gives me fast food gift certificates for Christmas.
My grandmother, whom I love dearly, is not well known for giving good gifts.

There are also other rules regarding "whom." For example, in prepositional phrases, one usually uses "whom" such as "to whom it may concern."

Exercise 2: A Pause for Comma and Her Friends

Students will often say that they do not have any idea how to put in commas, and their solution is to either omit them completely or use them obsessively. Neither "solution" is a good one. Frankly, the English language has so many rules for inserting commas that I cannot begin to cover them here. But what I can give you is something of a short cut. Below I have listed the six most common comma errors in essay writing. Learn these rules and then check your essay to make sure that you are not abusing and misusing the poor little misunderstood comma.

1. INTRODUCTORY ELEMENTS NEED COMMAS

Check every sentence and see if it begins with a subject. If not, check to see if the sentence begins with an introductory element. (An introductory element can be one single word, a phrase, or a clause that tells when, where, how, or why the main action of the sentence occurs.) If you have an introductory element, you will need a comma after it to separate it from the main part of the sentence.

You are probably thinking that if you don't have time to even call your grandmother back, then how will you have the time to check every sentence for this thing called an introductory element. Trust me on this. You will only have to do it once, and then it will be almost instinctive. So, give yourself fifteen minutes now and try it. If you need extra help, ask your professor or a tutor to give you fifteen minutes and practice on your essay.

Examples:

1. So, you want to be famous?
2. In fact, you can become famous if you learn how to place commas.
3. Since not many people know how to use commas, you can become famous for this bit of knowledge alone.

2. KILL THE RUN-ON SENTENCES

You have probably read on one of your essays that you had a run-on, and you wonder what is it that makes every professor pounce if you have just one. Well, run-on sentences are so easy to fix, it is a shame that they occur at all. If you ever turn in a resume to anyone who knows a little bit about grammar, they will know this rule—and so should you to avoid looking the fool.

To check for run-on sentences before someone else finds them for you, look for coordinating conjunctions in your sentences. (A coordinating conjunction is: and, but, or, nor, for, so, and yet.) If what is before and after the coordinating conjunction is a complete sentence, then you must use a comma before the coordinating conjunction.

Examples:

1. Fred had rebelled long enough about run-on sentences, and one day, he finally decided to learn what they were.
2. I gave the student a high grade, but I cautioned him that his grammar needed some work.

3. What's After That?

If you have an adjective clause beginning with "that" do not place a comma around the phrase. It's that simple.

Examples:

1. The belief that cats do not care for their owners is untrue to many a cat lover.
2. The park that I like to visit is becoming too crowded.

4. Three's a Crowd

If you have a series of three or more words, phrases, or clauses, you need commas separating each item in a series. There is some debate whether or not you need the comma for the last item in a series, but if you put one there, you are never wrong.

Examples:

1. The baby ate peas, beets, and creamed chicken.
2. The dark, muddy, twisting path led to a cave.
3. She has written the exam, copied it, and set it on her desk to hand out to the students.

5. Essential or Not Essential?

Young writers often think that every sentence that sounds like the following requires commas: Principals who have been convicted of any felony charge should lose their jobs.

In that sentence you should not set off any of the phrases with commas although many students want the sentence to read like this: Principals, who have been convicted of any felony charge, should lose their jobs.

Here is the rule. If adjective clauses beginning with *which, who, whom, whose, when,* or *where* are essential to understanding the sentence, then you do not set off that clause with commas. If it is unessential to the meaning of the sentence, then you would.

Examples:

1. The play *Rent* was wonderful. (I have to know that the play was *Rent* or else I would not understand the message of the sentence.)
2. Rent, the play, was the best performance I ever saw. (I do not have to know that Rent was a play to understand this sentence.)
   Remember this rule: Essential to the meaning = no comma. Non-essential to the meaning = a comma.

6. COMMA SPLICES

Comma splices are quite similar to run-on sentences in that two independent clauses have been incorrectly joined together. Essentially, the error with a comma splice is that you have incorrectly joined them with a comma, "splicing" them together.

So, how do you identify and fix the problem? First, look for independent clauses that can stand alone as two sentences but are written as one sentence with only a comma between them. Once you find a comma splice, you have many options on how to fix it. You may separate the clauses into two sentences. You may add a coordinating conjunction after the comma. You may use a semi-colon rather than a comma. Or you may rewrite the sentence so that you are changing one of the independent clauses to a dependent clause.

(The information from this chapter is derived from *The Everyday Writer* by Andrea Lunsford and Robert Connors; *The Elements of Style* by E.B. White and William Strunk, Jr.; *Words Fail Me* by Patricia T. O'Conner; and my mother, my first teacher, who fined me a quarter if I placed a preposition at the end of a sentence.)

35
Final Thoughts on Writing

When I was eighteen, I swore that I would never become an English teacher in any form: high school, college, or substitute. But here I am. At twenty, I swore I would never venture into a career as difficult and unstable as writing. But here I am. And what is more interesting: here I chose to be.

We never quite know the direction our lives will take and how much (or how little) writing will be involved. Whether it's for personal purposes, reports, or an annual Christmas letter, we will always strive to present our best thoughts on the page. E.B. White wrote that "writing itself is an act of faith, nothing else. And it must be the writer, above all others, who keeps it alive—choked with laughter, or with pain." White is correct in that it is each writer's responsibility to keep writing and to make the writing feel alive. Never can anyone do that job for us.

Writing will present challenges and celebrations, and we must accept both of those when we sit down to put our words on paper. The exercises in this book have provided many different techniques that we can use, but more importantly, the exercises have provided a strong sense of process and discovery. As we continue on our writing paths, may we enjoy all the steps and journeys that follow.